THE LORD'S SUPPER:

SEVEN MEANINGS

The Lord's Supper:

SEVEN MEANINGS

BY

HAROLD E. FEY

NEW YORK

HARPER & BROTHERS PUBLISHERS

To My Mother and My Father

CONTENTS

The principal references to the Lord's Supper in the New Testament, in the order in which they were written, are:

I Corinthians 11:17-34
Mark 14:22-25
Matthew 26:26-29
Luke 22:14-20
John 6:51-58

Other references to the Lord's Supper are:

Luke 24:30, 35
Acts 1:13; 2:42, 46-47; 20:7, 11; 27:35
I Corinthians 5:7; 10:1-4, 16-22; 12:11-13
Hebrews 13:10
II Peter 2:13
I John 5:6, 8
Jude verse 12
Revelation 19:7, 9

Scripture quotations in this book are taken from the Revised Standard Version of the New Testament, issued in 1946, and are cited by permission of the International Council of Religious Education and of Thomas Nelson & Sons.

THE LORD'S SUPPER:

SEVEN MEANINGS

Ye who do truly and earnestly repent you of your sins and are in love and charity with your neighbors and intend to lead a new life, following the commandments of God and walking from henceforth in his holy ways; draw near with faith and take this holy sacrament to your comfort; and make your humble confession to Almighty God, devoutly kneeling.

BOOK OF COMMON PRAYER

CHAPTER ONE

The Language of the Soul

THE LANGUAGE of the soul is a language of deeds as well as words. It speaks through both deeds and words in the act of worship which constitutes its highest and noblest expression. This act is variously known as the Lord's Supper, the Eucharist or the Holy Communion. It was begun by Jesus Christ.

As the time approached for his death, Jesus arranged for a last repast with his disciples. During the course of this meal he took the food and the drink which were most commonly found on Palestinian tables and asked his disciples to think of them henceforth as carrying new meanings.

According to Paul, who wrote the earliest New Testament account about 54 A.D., this is what happened: "The Lord Jesus on the night when he was betrayed took bread, and when he had given thanks, he broke it, and said, 'This is my body which is broken for you. Do this in remembrance of me.' In the same way also the cup, after supper, saying, 'This cup is the new covenant in my blood. Do this, as often as you drink it, in remembrance of me.' For as often as you eat this bread and drink this cup, you proclaim the Lord's death until he comes" (I Cor. 11:23b-27).

The Gospel accounts which were written later add little to this extraordinarily simple statement, which was set down

3

approximately twenty years after the event. They give a few
additional details, some of which support and some of which
differ from this story. They reveal how shameful was the sin
of Judas, whose betrayal is set against the sad intimacy of this
fateful farewell. We are helped to understand, but not too
clearly, that there may have been some relation between the
Last Supper and the Passover. Echoing through the hush of a
Judean evening in spring, we hear the sound of a hymn whose
words we shall never know in this life. We ask ourselves who
was the nameless friend who provided the upper room. Matthew, Mark and Luke all tell us that Jesus said that henceforth
he would not drink of the fruit of the vine "until the kingdom
of God shall come," as Luke phrases it. But so far as the
essential nature of this act of worship is concerned, it is all
stated in the eighty-nine words of the English text as quoted
from Paul.

As usual, the brevity of the New Testament record leaves
us with some questions that cannot be answered with absolute
certainty. While they do not invalidate the central core of
meaning which we may legitimately find in the Lord's Supper,
these questions must not be forgotten. Their existence should
temper any tendency to revive the dogmatism which has
blighted the church's observance of this memorial for the last
thousand years.

The central question is whether Jesus *ordered* his disciples
to observe this rite and whether he meant that his order should
henceforth always be obeyed. The words which Paul quotes
from Jesus are a command, at least to those who were present.
The undeviating practice of the church from the earliest times
supports the view that they were accepted as such from the
beginning. But Paul was not present in the upper room, and

the statement which is found in Mark, the earliest of the Gospels, is not so clearly a command. None of the accounts prescribes the manner or the frequency of the observance. Matthew follows closely the account as it appears in Mark. Luke is confused, either placing the offering of the wine first or presenting it as offered twice. John so completely spiritualizes his account that he omits to describe the inauguration. His language which was probably but not certainly intended to refer to the communion is unilluminating on this point.

In the light of the condition of the scriptural record and of what we know of the spirit and purpose of Jesus in other connections, we inquire what meaning Jesus intended to convey in the upper room. The simplest explanation is likely to be the truest: that Jesus was attempting to teach an important truth or truths by an easily remembered parable. Jewish history was full of prophets who used object lessons as a means of instruction. Their acted parables constituted a fundamental element in the religious teaching which Jesus, along with others of his contemporaries, studied in the synagogue.

Jesus had repeatedly attempted to prepare the disciples for his death. What would be more natural than that, as the end neared, the Master should make one more attempt to explain the meaning of his decision? Taking bread and wine, without which no meal was complete, he made them the symbols of what he was about to offer in a "last full measure of devotion." He asked his beloved associates to use them to remember him at future meals like those he had shared with them so often. On what occasion would gratitude to God more spontaneously rise to their minds? When could they better deepen their own fellowship or celebrate their faith in the inevitable victory of the coming kingdom?

The symbols of this parable were already invested with many associations for the disciples. They were elements in the daily meals of even the poor, among whom the followers of Jesus were numbered. So it was only natural that the Eucharist should become at first a part of a common meal or "love feast" of the Christian community. It was probably not observed separately until the second century. The elements of the communion were used also in the familiar ritual meals of the Jewish faith. The most common of these was the *kiddush* (also spelled *quiddush*), a domestic ceremony observed on the evening of each Sabbath or feast day. The act of sanctification of the day was preceded by a social meal during which bread and wine were solemnly blessed and distributed to the household. Since Jesus and his disciples were a *chaburoth* or group of friends who met together to discuss religion, as other groups did in his day, they had often observed this ceremony together.

So the "acted parable" of the Lord's Supper was not a novel experience to the disciples. That fact added to its meaning. In this observance Jesus brought consolation to his disciples by overlaying a familiar association with new significance. He "summed up and perpetuated that relationship with him which had been theirs in the days of his ministry," as Hugh Watt says.* He also provided them with a key to the understanding of questions which would hardly sink deep into their minds until he had made the supreme sacrifice. But when they attempted to appropriate as their own the meaning of his life, death and resurrection, re-enactment of the simple drama of the upper room would become a sacrament of deliverance and of unbelievable joy.

* Article "Eucharist," *Encyclopedia of Religion and Ethics,* edited by James Hastings (New York: Charles Scribner's Sons, 1912).

Much ensued from the events of that night in the upper room. It is not irreverent to reflect on what Christian history might have been had no last supper preceded Gethsemane and Calvary. Soon generations arose who knew not Jesus or the apostles. Long ages impended in which Western civilization reached a very low level. The time would soon come when the number of Christians who valued or could read the written record of the life of Christ and the beginnings of the Christian community would be small indeed. But the plain words of Jesus at the Last Supper lived on in the corporate memory of the church.

The recurring drama of commemoration kept alive their meaning. Even though the crass superstition of dark and ignorant centuries corrupted the purpose behind the words, the observance of the Lord's Supper provided a nucleus around which the Christian community could rally for the worship of God until a more luminous day would break with the Reformation. Without the continuing observance of this central act of devotion, the church might have departed even farther than it did from the vision of its founder. It might not have survived as the Christian Church.

That it did survive is a fact for which we can never be sufficiently grateful. It gives us courage at a time when civilization itself is again in peril. It gives us confidence in the mission of the fellowship of believers and in the abiding strength of the Spirit of God among men in a changing world.

It is useless to pretend that the recovery of the meaning of the Lord's Supper is the whole answer to Christendom's inner weakness. Our nationalistic and sectarian pride, our little faith and large greed, our disunity, lack of vision and insensitivity to both the sufferings of humanity and the movement of the

Spirit of God in our time will not so easily fall away. But the fact that the Protestant observance of the Lord's Supper is largely sterile, ritualistic and unintelligent, that the Roman Catholic mass is thickly encrusted with superstition and materialism, that the Eastern churches still seek to propitiate God with an offering dominated by the barbaric theology of the days of Charlemagne, is not unrelated to the low state of spiritual health which marks present-day Christianity.

Once a church which possessed no paid ministry, no priesthood, no cathedrals or church buildings, no endowments, no salaried bishops or secretaries, and no publicity except the lies told by its enemies, held a disintegrating world together and laid the basis of a new civilization. Its power was not its own. What it had was a gift. The gift was given it in meetings of little groups who assembled before dawn in houses on back streets and in caves under Rome. Those who gathered heard sermons only infrequently, when men like Paul the sail-maker came their way. But whenever they met they broke bread with gladness and singleness of heart and shared the cup of their covenant with Christ. What did that church have that we do not have today?

I . . . exhort you to have but one faith, and one preaching and one Eucharist. For there is one flesh of the Lord Jesus Christ, and his blood which was shed for us is one; one loaf also is broken to all and one cup is distributed among them all.

IGNATIUS in his letter to the Philadelphians, 110 A. D.

CHAPTER TWO

Names of the Communion

"WHEN YOU SEE alabaster gleaming in refulgent purity, remember the body broken for you. In frankincense and myrrh illuminated by the fire of rubies, pledge the new testament in my blood." Jesus did not say that, but why didn't he say something like it? Why did not the Master choose a costly memorial? His followers would have hesitated at no sacrifice. He might have reasoned that something inaccessible and infinitely precious would best symbolize the inexpressible worth of the life of the Son of God. Instead he took the two commonest elements of every Palestinian meal and made them his monument.

The reason must have been that he sought a symbol which was in the reach of everybody. Nobody was so poor that he did not have bread and wine. The bread might be like stone, and it often was, but it was bread. The wine might be the sharp, acrid drink of the poorest farmer, but even if it was poured out of a rotting wineskin it would serve in that land of spare wells to refresh the body. How often had Jesus and his band of faithful men eaten meals which were nothing more than just bread and wine. He would dare to use them as his memorial! So the monument was erected, to stand through succeeding centuries. Its grandeur, beauty and healing strength have ever since made it the central act of Christian worship.

The names by which this memorial has come to be known in various lands and in differing times offer something of a clue to its richness of meaning to the Christians of these many generations. From the first the term "the Lord's Supper" has been universally understood. It follows in direct succession upon that meal in the upper room when the shadow of the cross loomed so terribly near. It is the name by which nearly all Protestant Christians know this act of worship. It speaks of the living fellowship of Christ with the believer. He is still the host at the head of the table. His are the hands which break the bread and pass the cup. His is the voice pledging the new covenant in his blood. He is present as he was in the upper room, not in the bread and wine, but as the Living Presence standing beside every believer and giving the symbols their overflowing and imperishable meaning.

Another historic name is "the Eucharist." The word is from the Greek. It means "thanksgiving." It was probably the Greek equivalent of the Jewish *barakhah* in which God's blessing was asked at the beginning of a meal. The Roman Catholic and other churches use "Eucharist" to designate the Lord's Supper. There are some who claim that the word is associated with the particular interpretation which the Roman Church puts upon the mass. This claim is without foundation in fact. "Eucharist" was one of the terms used in the earliest documents for the common meal or "love feast" of the early Christian community to suggest that the meal had been blessed by Christ. Later in the second century it was used to refer especially to the bread and wine of the Lord's Supper. Neither in its intrinsic meaning nor in its history is there any reason why Protestants may not also use this name, if they care to do so. It is full of the grace of gratitude, an essential part of the significance of the memorial.

Another common term is "the Communion," or "the Holy Communion." This term is used by many in the Protestant Episcopal Church and by a large number of others. "Communion" derives from Latin words meaning sharing together a service, office, function or duty. It refers here to the fact that at the Lord's Supper the believer does not feast alone, but in fellowship with Christ. The unity of the Christian and his Savior is celebrated and strengthened in this act of worship. But this is not all. From the beginning among the twelve disciples it has also provided a reaffirmation of the unity of believers with one another in the church. As often as Christians partake of these symbols, they bear witness to the fact that the unity of the church can be found only in its Head. In the church's present scandalously divided state, we also confess that its divisions exist because too often we have forgotten who its Head is.

These three are the terms with which we are most familiar, but they by no means exhaust the rich variety of names by which the Eucharist is designated. The great churches of the Eastern tradition—the Greek and Russian Orthodox—refer to it most often as "the Divine Liturgy." Taking their understanding of it from John of Damascus (died about 759), these churches regard the observance as "the pre-eminent public service offered to God by the Christian society." They hold, as does the Roman Catholic Church, that during the communion service the priest invokes divine power to work a miracle converting the bread and wine into the actual body and blood of Christ. The priest and the people therefore are engaged in an act of worship in which the sacrifice of Christ is re-enacted. Hence the term, "the Divine Liturgy." The commonly accepted doctrine is that the offering of the actual body and blood of Christ reminds God of his obligation to sinners. Because of the merits of Christ, God restrains his wrath and forgives sinners.

The Roman Catholic Church refers to the entire service which has been built around the communion as "the mass." The word comes from the Latin *mittere*, to send. Its use arose with the practice of dismissing the catechumens and others at a certain point in the service, for only baptized believers might partake of the communion. The first record of its use is in the third century. The term from which "mass" comes originally referred to any act of dismissal, including the word spoken by an official ending a public meeting. Its meaning is connected with the communion only by usage. It does however point to the fact that this act of worship is reserved for those who openly confess Christ as their Savior.

The Syriac-speaking, Coptic and Armenian churches refer to the Lord's Supper as "the Oblation" or "the Present." Like the Eastern churches, under whose influence they have long stood, they regard the observance as an offering, something which the worshiper does for God, but for his own ends. They hold that God must be propitiated. The divine sacrifice, the body and blood of Christ, is an efficacious offering for this purpose. By this present they appease God and earn merit for themselves. The only element of truth which an American Protestant can find in this conception is that in partaking of the Lord's Supper we "do show forth the Lord's death until he comes." We bear our witness to His living presence, not only at communion but always, but we are under no illusions that by so doing we put God under obligation.

Much more congenial to our views is the term by which the Abyssinian or Ethiopian Church designates the Eucharist. This church, which is very ancient, refers to it as "the Consecration." Not only are the elements consecrated but, much more important, the believers who partake of them make or renew their covenant with Christ. No communion service which is not an act of personal and corporate rededication is worthy of the name. Consecration in this connection means that the person consecrated is set apart as sacred, being wholly reserved and committed. This note might appear with spiritual profit in far more of our observances.

The early Christian community used the term "agape" or "love feast" to cover both the fellowship meal and the observance of the Lord's Supper. Since both were regular observances of the early church, and nearly always came together, it was not until several generations had passed that they were distinguished by different names. But we today would gain if we recognized more often that the true communion is always a love feast. The members of the Christian community are bound to each other and to their Lord by unbreakable bonds. In each communion service we reaffirm our community with those who met, usually before day, in the catacombs and elsewhere, to celebrate the love of God and to strengthen their bonds with one another.

"The blessed sacrament of the altar" was the term employed by Augustine (died 430) to designate the Lord's Supper. "The breaking of bread," a New Testament phrase for the observance, continues to be used to this day. The communion is often referred to as "the table of the Lord," a designation which has much the same significance as "Lord's Supper." "Eulogio" or "the Blessing" was once used, but has now been superseded by the more euphonious "Eucharist." "Synaxis" or "the Assembly," "the Holy of Holies" and "the Lord's Body" are terms which were used by some churches for a time but have now become obsolete.

Each of these sixteen terms is a facet, more or less brilliant, of a luminous jewel. Taken together, they throw light on the meaning of the principal act of worship of the Christian faith.

And after we have thus [in baptism] bathed the person who has become a believer and an adherent, we lead him to the brethren, as they are called, where they are assembled to offer up common prayers on behalf of themselves and the newly enlightened one and all others everywhere, that it may be vouchsafed to us who have learned the truth to be found also in our conduct good members of the society and keepers of the commandments, that we may be saved with the eternal salvation. Then when we have done our prayers, we greet one another with a kiss. Then there is presented to the president of the brethren a loaf and a cup of water and wine and he, after taking them, offers up praise and glory to the Father of all things, through the name of the Son and the Holy Ghost; and he gives thanks at length for these favors of God to us. And when he has ended the prayers and the thanksgiving (Eucharist), the whole assistant people present assent with an "Amen"—the Hebrew word meaning "So be it!"

And when the president has given thanks and the whole people have assented, those who are called deacons (ministers) among us receive a portion of the loaf and wine and water, over which the thanksgiving has been made, to each of those who are present, and they take it away to those who are not. And this food is called among us the Eucharist; and no one is allowed to partake of it unless he believes that what we teach is true and has been washed in the laver for the remission of sins and for regeneration and is living as Christ enjoined. For we do not receive these things as common bread or common drink, but just as Jesus Christ our Savior, by the word of God made flesh, had both flesh and blood for our salvation, so we have been taught that the food over which thanks have been given by the word of prayer comes from him—that food from which our blood and our flesh are by assimilation nourished—is both the flesh and blood of that Jesus Christ who was made flesh. For the Apostles delivered in the memoirs compiled by them, which are called Gospels, that this command was given to them— that Jesus took bread.

JUSTIN MARTYR (120-165 A.D.) in
his Apology addressed to Emperor Antoninus Pius

CHAPTER THREE

Seven Meanings

IF IT BE granted that the Lord's Supper is the great classic of the language of the soul, what are its meanings? If it is a means of grace, through which we can come to a more perfect understanding of the love and majesty of God, how may we explore its riches? Even though we may not presume to scale to their tops the peaks of God's perfect wisdom, we may look upon his lofty ranges and distinguish one mountain from another. We may even climb each a little way and survey from a higher vantage point the glory of his creation and the magnificent sweep of his purposes.

The New Testament accounts of its institution give no indication that the Lord's Supper was originally intended to be clothed in mystery. The grace of God, which is mediated through the communion, is a mystery. But the observance itself can be understood by a child. Its meanings should therefore be capable of simple statement. Such statement should be attempted in every church, so that Christians will be encouraged to come with illumined faith to the table of the Lord, where the bread of life is spread for all who believe. It need not preclude or rule out the profound analysis and the sharp distinctions of scholarship. On the other hand, it will proceed on the assumption that scholarship worthy of the name desires that every follower of Christ shall have at least an elementary understanding of the Lord's Supper.

Reduced to most elemental terms, all the New Testament accounts of the inauguration of the Lord's Supper agree that it contained three elements. The first was thanksgiving to God. The second was remembrance of Jesus Christ and of the redemptive quality of his sacrifice. The third was the grateful reception by the disciples of the symbols of the life that was in Christ, their act sealing a covenant with him.

In addition to these three elements which they share with Paul, the Synoptic Gospels make it appear that the rite was an anticipation of the coming victory of the Messiah. All emphasize the brotherly fellowship which bound the disciples together in a common loyalty whose center was Christ. Matthew declares that the "blood of the covenant" is "poured out for many unto remission of sins." All the Synoptics imply the assurance of immortality both in Jesus and on the part of those who covenant with him.

To most Protestants, the first meaning of the communion is that it is a memorial to Jesus Christ. The fact that many never go beyond this idea should not minimize its significance for a living faith. The truth that Jesus Christ lived is the most important truth in human history. From it all other events take their meaning. In the symbols of his body and blood, his identification with our humanity is recalled. We see him not as a high priest who cannot be touched with the feeling of our infirmities, but as one of ourselves, tempted in all points as we are, yet without sin.

Most of our hymns celebrate the Lord's Supper as an act of remembrance. But too many of them, like most prayers before communion, make this a remembrance of something

far away and long ago. Jesus is definitely dead. His blood is
a red stain on the ground beneath the cross. His body is a
bruised and lifeless corpse which must quickly be buried. The
memorial we raise to Jesus in such ways had better never be
raised. Jesus is alive. He must be remembered as living. The
Christians whom Pliny in his letter to Trajan (97 A.D.)
described as gathering before dawn and singing a hymn to
Christ and pledging themselves by a sacrament "to abstain
from certain crimes" were not raising a gravestone over a
vanished leader. When they remembered Jesus, he was there
with them. The Eucharist perpetuated his relationship with
them.

A second meaning of the Lord's Supper is that contained
in the term, "the Eucharist." From the earliest times it was a
joyous thanksgiving. The *Didache,* which was written about
100 A.D., uses "thank offering" and "breaking of bread"
synonymously in describing the Lord's Supper. Here the
radiant joy which sent the early church singing through the
Mediterranean world had its birth. Here it must have its
resurrection. The disciples broke bread "with gladness and
singleness of heart, praising God and having favor with all
the people" (Acts 2:46-47). Who has greater occasion for
gratitude than the Christian, for whom the Eucharist has
always been reserved? Who has more fundamental reason
for optimism, for courage in the face of death and destruction,
for faith in the power of Christian life to endure and triumph?
We offer thanks to God for a redemption which is a present
fact as well as a future hope, for a Redeemer who brought
divinity to our common life.

A third, meaning of the Lord's Supper is found in the
covenant which it represents between the living Christ and

those who take part in this act. The wine, Jesus said, is "my blood of the covenant." Again it was referred to as "the new covenant in my blood." The disciples discarded the old compact by which Jews were bound and entered into this new relationship. As Jews they would feel themselves sacredly bound by the new pledge, which like the old was unto death. The good faith of the proposer of the covenant was soon eternally confirmed by the cross. The act of communion is still a new commitment to the way of the cross.

It is this ethical commitment which should forever dissociate the observance of the Lord's Supper from the realm of magic. It requires the participant to look within if there is any evil thing in him and to seek penitently for a clean heart and a right spirit. It requires him who administers the communion to look closely to his own life lest he prove to be an unworthy minister. When the people of the Mediterranean world took knowledge of the disciples that they had been with Jesus, the thing that excited their wonder was an observable change in the spirit and behavior of these former nondescripts. Their participation in a new and what seemed a mysterious rite was known but it was regarded as incidental.

The Eucharist is in the fourth place an affirmation and renewal of the fellowship of the believer with Christ and with his church. Paul was the great exponent of the idea that the church is the body of Christ. "For just as the body is one and has many members, and all the members of the body, though many, are one body, so it is with Christ," he said. "For by one Spirit we were all baptized into one body—Jews or Greeks, slaves or free—and all were made to drink of one Spirit. For the body does not consist of one member but of many" (I Cor. 12:12-14).

In the Lord's Supper we affirm the fact of the communion of the church with its living Head and with the ecumenical body of believers throughout the world. We enter into the heritage of the early Christian Church, whose chief act of worship from the first was the breaking of bread in the Lord's Supper. When we recall the tremendous spiritual drive of that church, which seldom heard a sermon but never missed a communion, we are compelled to reflect whether a church has done its whole duty to God when it has listened to an eloquent preacher.

A fifth meaning of the Eucharist is that the source of spiritual strength is in God. In the Lord's Supper the believer is fed, and not by himself. The bread and the wine are the free gift of God "for the nourishment of the soul," as Harnack says. Paul referred to these representative symbols as "spiritual food" and "spiritual drink." In themselves they are bread and wine—nothing more. All the intricate theories of Scholasticism concerning transubstantiation have not in a thousand years made anything more of them than bread and wine. Their effect on the one who eats and drinks is exactly the effect of any other like amount of these substances. But if they are partaken of with faith by a person who recognizes in them a symbol of the desire and purpose of God spiritually to sustain his children, they will be a means of grace. It is the faith that God the Father watches over and desires to nourish his family unto all good works which is necessary. God does not disappoint those who thus express their prayer for nurture.

A sixth meaning of the Lord's Supper is its representation of the atonement. The ministry of reconciliation is here re-enacted. Only thus can the presence of Judas at the Last Supper be explained. Until the end the opportunity for forgiveness was held out to this sinner. Although Judas turned away, the triumph of reconciliation is shown by the fact that the eleven remained. They too were on the verge of estrangement, were more concerned with personal advantage than with the kingdom of God. The Last Supper represented the healing of wounds and the cauterizing of cancerous jealousies. It is still a place where penitent men and women can find forgiveness and at-one-ment with the Father.

Finally, in the Lord's Supper we celebrate the fact and declare the hope of immortality. Jesus was confident that his death could and would be overcome by the power of God. If the temple were torn down, in three days it would be erected again. God would not fail in the ultimate test. Evil could be overcome, and be overcome with good. God could be trusted. Men who steadfastly act in the faith that God is love will not be let down. Even though they lay down their lives, they will receive them again. This is what happened. Jesus, who was crucified, lived again. After Easter flung into the sky the banners of her eternal dawn, all who observed the Lord's Supper "proclaimed," in the words of Paul, "the Lord's death until he comes." Jesus, who was risen, was alive again.

The early Christian community had a pressing and eager hope of Christ's personal and bodily reappearance. When it became apparent that the kingdom of God actually was within them, that they need not keep eyes fixed on the heavens waiting for a Presence which was already in their midst, they held triumphantly to the faith that in his enlarged life they too, in some way they could not clearly define, shared and would continue to share. The sacrament of deliverance stretched beyond this life. The secret of their courage

lay in their conviction that they need not fear even the last
enemy, death. That too had been put under foot. Now at last
they were really free.

Here then are seven meanings of this great classic of the
language of the soul. There may be others. These seven may
be stated differently and with more insight. But each of these
seven meanings lies within an area of significance which is
worth further exploration. This we shall attempt, taking
account of some of the historic controversies which have at
times risen and waned over certain problems of the Eucharist.
Here the effort is simply to survey in one panoramic view a
territory which will richly reward detailed exploration.

At no time, however, must we allow ourselves to forget
that in the communion we re-enact the divine drama of redemption. We become a part of that incredible story. Through
it we are lifted out of our time-bound lives. Once again the
light shines around a tall figure in an upper room and we are
there crying with the rest: "Lord, is it I? Is it I?" The light
fades and we hear the echoes of Gethsemane at night, riven
with the agony of unanswered prayer. The darkness piles
mountain-high and becomes a Golgotha, pierced with a cry
from a cross. It yields to an unbelievable dawn shining above
an empty tomb. It ends in a gasp of surprise as we break
bread on the Emmaus Road. We have walked with Jesus,
who, being dead, yet lives.

I believe that in the holy Eucharist—i.e., the supper of thanksgiving—the true body of Christ is present by the contemplation of faith; i.e., that they who thank the Lord for the kindness conferred on us in his Son acknowledge that he assumed true flesh, in it truly suffered, truly washed away our sins in his own blood; that thus everything done by Christ becomes present to them by contemplation of faith. But that the body of Christ in essence and reality—i.e., the natural body itself—is either present in the supper or is masticated by our teeth, as the Papists and some who long for the flesh-pots of Egypt assert, we not only deny but firmly maintain is an error opposed to God's word.

HULDRICH ZWINGLI in his confession
of faith before Emperor Charles V
at the Diet of Augsburg, 1530

At least once every week the table of the Lord ought to have been spread before each congregation of Christians, and the promises to have been declared for their spiritual nourishment; no person ought to have been compelled to partake, but all ought to have been exhorted and stimulated, and those who were negligent to have been reproved.

JOHN CALVIN in the *Institutes*

Luther disapproved of the daily celebration of the Mass, because it had become customary to celebrate it without communication on the part of the lay people. But he heartily advocated the restoration of the Holy Communion as the normal worship of the congregation on the Lord's Day and on the great festivals of the church year. The determination of Luther to retain the Eucharist as the norm of worship was so strong that the Lutheran churches in Germany continued without a break to worship in this historic way until about the year 1722, when the acids of rationalism and the salves of pietism began to be applied in alternate doses to an ailing church.

SCOTT FRANCIS BRENNER in *The Way of Worship* (New York: The Macmillan Company, 1944), page 75

CHAPTER FOUR

In Remembrance of Me

Take, eat; this is my body which is broken for you: this do in remembrance of me. This cup is the new testament in my blood: this do ye, as oft as ye drink it, in remembrance of me.
— *I Corinthians 11:24-25*

THE ABOVE WORDS were read at the first evangelical communion service which was held in the great minster in Zurich on Thursday, April 13, 1525. It was presided over by Huldrich Zwingli. This Swiss reformer refused to join Luther in the impossible attempt to compromise with Catholic superstition concerning the mass. He held that Christ is present in the Lord's Supper only to those who wait for him in faith. For several years he had taught thus. However, it was not until the town council of Zurich was ready to give its cordial approval that he acted to change the observance. The decision was a fateful one and was not to be taken hastily. It might bring war against the city. It might result in Zwingli's being burned at the stake. But now both he and the council were ready. A week in advance he published the order of service for an observance of the Lord's Supper like none that had ever been held in Zurich.

As the citizens of the town crowded into the great minster

they saw in the nave tables covered with clean linen cloth. On the tables were great platters filled with unleavened bread and wooden beakers full of wine. Zwingli entered the pulpit and preached a sermon. The bread, he said, was a symbol. Those who would take it in faith would commune with Christ. The wine too was a symbol. It would not be withheld, as the Roman Catholic custom was, but would be distributed to laity and clergy alike as a representation of the blood of the covenant with Christ. The congregation knelt as the preacher led them in prayer.

Then a deacon read the account containing the above words, beginning with the twentieth verse of I Corinthians 11. Zwingli and the congregation next participated in the liturgy he had written. It was in the language of the people. It omitted the Latin which nobody understood. It excluded the music which was believed to be not in accordance with the New Testament. The teaching concerning transubstantiation which was in the Catholic liturgy was conspicuous by its absence. The early Palestinian simplicity of the Last Supper again became a reality as the deacons passed the elements to the congregation, which was divided with the men on one side and the women on the other. The service made a great impression. It was repeated on the two following days and thereafter each Sunday. Later the altar of the great minster was removed, since the elimination of sacrifice had made it meaningless, and the organ was taken out, "since there was no longer to be music in the churches."

This first post-medieval communion service was one of the decisive events of the Protestant Reformation. It might be called the beginning of the Reformation in so far as it repre-sented a thoroughgoing repudiation of the superstitions which had accumulated for centuries in the Catholic ritual. Zwingli's view, as he stated it five years later in his confession of faith made before Emperor Charles V at the Diet of Augsburg, was: "I believe that in the holy Eucharist—i.e., the supper of thanksgiving—the true body of Christ is present by the contemplation of faith; i.e., that they who thank the Lord for the kindness conferred on us in his Son acknowledge that he assumed true flesh, in it truly suffered, truly washed away our sins in his own blood, and thus everything done by Christ becomes present to them by contemplation of faith. But that the body of Christ in essence and reality—i.e., the natural body itself—is either present in the supper or is masticated by our teeth, as the Papists and some who long for the fleshpots of Egypt assert, we not only deny but firmly maintain is an error opposed to God's word."

The Protestant Reformation accomplished nothing so important as its rediscovery of Jesus Christ. It is commonly recognized that this occurred when Luther opened the Bible to the people. This is true but not the whole truth. Zwingli's recovery of the Lord's Supper in its New Testament simplicity was also an important step in this direction. The remembrance of Christ was reborn. He was no longer a name given to a species of magic by which sins were forgiven without repentance. He became once more the Son of God, who had lived in history, had taught men to have faith in God, their Father in heaven, had suffered, died and risen again. He lived, and any believer who had faith might commune with him and find forgiveness, peace and power. Today, thanks to Zwingli, we do not have to unearth Christ from beneath the accumulation of centuries of magic and superstition which is the Roman Catholic mass.

"This do in remembrance of me." What were the disciples to remember? Jesus had been their teacher and leader during the entire period of his public ministry. Much had happened during that time; much had been said. Was there a principle of selection, a hierarchy of value? The writer of John's Gospel declared that there was. In chapters 13 to 18 he repeats the teaching which that part of the church living under the Greek influence at the end of the first Christian century believed was given at the Last Supper. These chapters contain the great parable of the vine and the branches and the prayer of Jesus for the preservation and unity of "those whom thou hast given me." *The integrity of the Christian community* is the theme of both the parable and the prayer. It was uppermost in the mind of the church when John's Gospel was written at the end of the second generation after the crucifixion.

Paul and the writers of the Synoptic Gospels, who wrote much closer to the event, made no reference to this teaching as set down in John's Gospel. According to them, Jesus simply gave the twelve disciples a thing to do and asked them to do it in remembrance of him. But the contradiction between them and the later writer may not be so great as an unreflective reading of the records might make it appear. This becomes plain when we recall that the words concerning remembrance were not spoken in general. "This is my body . . . This is the new covenant in my blood," Jesus had said. It was these representative symbols which were to channel the disciples' remembrance.

Remember me, Jesus seemed to be saying, as one of yourselves. Remember me as a man like you with a body which can suffer, grow weary, die. Remember our fellowship together, our sleeping and waking, our meals like this one in

happier days, our conversations by the seaside, our visits to
Zaccheus and to the home of Mary and Martha. Remember
me as a Jew, of the seed of David, who has in many an encounter broken with the leaders of his people and started a
new community which has taken up the mission Israel has
abandoned and undertaken the reconciliation of the world to
God. Remember me as the cornerstone which God is laying
in the new temple of which you yourselves are the living
stones. "This is my body which is broken for you. Do this in
remembrance of me."

Remember too, Jesus seemed to be saying, that I am
shedding my blood. I am going before you and laying down
my life. No person clothed with mortality can do more than
that. But this act is a testament, a pledge, a covenant. It is a
testament of love, a pledge of loyalty, a covenant of constancy
forever. In performing it you are binding yourselves. You are
taking upon yourselves my mission. You undertake it in my
faith that our heavenly Father will not desert you but will
bear you up and glorify his name with your victory. So you
bear your witness for the salvation of the world. "This cup
is the new covenant in my blood. Do this, as often as you
drink it, in remembrance of me."

Jesus was asking his disciples to remember him, then, first
as one who found a place in history. There in their land and
then in their time he had lived, moved and had his being.
God had been so richly present in him that they came to
believe that he was the heaven-sent Messiah, but this was
not to obscure the prior fact that this incredible being was
one of themselves. His village was known, his family was
known, his years of quiet labor in Joseph's carpenter shop
were known. Remember me, Jesus might have said, and

discover in history the true meaning of existence. In me you can glimpse a new dimension for your own lives and for all mankind.

In the second place, Jesus was asking them to remember him as the center of their communal life. He was the vine, they were the branches. Their lives were inextricably united. But they did not live unto themselves. The most important thing about this vine was its caretaker. God was the husbandman. He expected it to bear fruit. He stripped off the sterile branches. He pruned those that bore fruit so they would bear a larger crop. "If you abide in me, and my words abide in you, ask whatever you will and it shall be done for you" (John 15:7). They were the church of the living God, the community of the fruitful, the living organism through which the life of heaven flowed to mankind.

The remembrance of Jesus as the living Son of God was largely extinct in the church of the Middle Ages—how nearly dead is shown by the churches of Rome, which were almost all built by this time. Of the 433 churches and chapels in what was then the principal city of Christendom, only 15 were dedicated to Jesus, while no less than 121 were dedicated to Mary. Ignatius Loyola and some other medieval Catholics even went so far as to teach that in the Eucharist the flesh of Mary as well as that of Jesus was eaten. The Eucharist itself was interpreted in such a way as effectively to cause the Christian community to forget the Jesus of history and of the church.

The Reformation ended this state of affairs. It brought a part of the church at least to rediscover the purpose of Jesus in instituting the supper. Adolf Harnack described that purpose for us all: "By teaching them to think of him and of his death in the breaking of bread and the drinking of wine, and by saying of his death that it takes place for the remission of sins, he has claimed as his due from all future disciples what was a matter of course so long as he sojourned with them but might fade away after he was parted from them."

The Country Parson, being to administer the Sacraments, is at a stand with himself how or what behavior to assume for so holy things. Especially at Communion times he is in great confusion, as being not only to receive God, but to break and administer him. Neither finds he any issue in this but to throw himself down at the throne of grace, saying, "Lord, thou knowest what thou didst when thou appointedst it to be done thus: therefore do thou fulfil what thou didst appoint; for thou art not only the feast but the way to it."

GEORGE HERBERT, rector of Bremerton, Scotland, in the early 17th century, in *A Priest to the Temple*

But what if a man, seeing his sin, earnestly desire to hate it? Shall he not at the altar offer up at once his desire and the yet lingering sin and seek for strength? Is not this sacrament medicine as well as food? Is it an end only and not likewise the means? Is it merely a triumphant feast or is it not even more truly a blessed refreshment for and during the conflict?

SAMUEL TAYLOR COLERIDGE (1772-1834)

CHAPTER FIVE

In Thanksgiving to God

And day by day, attending the temple together
and breaking bread in their homes, they partook of
food with glad and generous hearts, praising God
and having favor with all the people.
— Acts 2:46-47

TWO EXTREMES of emphasis mark the history of the observance of the Lord's Supper. The Roman Catholic mass overstressed the element of sacrifice. The Protestant Reformation laid all its accent on the communion of the individual worshiper with the divine. Both minimized the eucharistic significance of the rite. Yet in the early church, thanksgiving was the primary and central meaning of the Lord's Supper. Collectively the church offered an overflowing sacrament of praise to God for Jesus Christ. His conversation, his daily walk, his little personal deeds of love, his luminous understanding, his parables, his acts of compassion, his bearing in the face of evil, his courage when confronted with the cross, his magnanimity in death, his tenderness in triumph at Easter—all were hymned with gratitude.

The spirit which has been described as "the lost radiance of the Christian religion" may be recovered at the communion table, where it was lost when the church allowed other emphases to take the place of the corporate act of praise which had been known from the beginning as the Eucharist. Immediately after the first Pentecost, the mood of sadness and foreboding which pervaded the upper room vanished. Before the open tomb, in the breaking of bread on the Emmaus Road and in other events the disciples discovered that Christ was victor over death. The white light of this tremendous fact suddenly illumined everything he had ever said or done. It shone on the disciples' own lives as they "returned to Jerusalem with great joy, and were continually in the temple blessing God."

Henceforth the disciples offered thanks to God not only because praise was integral to the Jewish worship to which they were accustomed or because the grace of gratitude had suffused the life and language of Jesus. Now they had a special and powerful reason of their own. God had given them through his Son the gift of new life. How then was it possible to gather about a table, as they had so often done with Jesus, without breaking into thanksgiving? No wonder these assemblies of the early church became known as love feasts! Here the disciples were returned to the presence of him whose birth set the angels singing. His continuing life after death made humanity echo their hallelujah chorus. So from the beginning the rite became "the thanksgiving," and the word Eucharist has been carried over into a number of languages.

This gratitude and joy are evident in one of the earliest communion prayers, which is recorded in the *Didache* or *Teaching of the Apostles* (written about 100 A.D.). Part of the prayer, which includes instructions for the observance, follows:

"Now with regard to the Thanksgiving (Eucharist) thus give ye thanks. First concerning the cup.

"We give thanks to Thee, our Father, for the holy vine of David Thy servant, which Thou didst make known unto us through Jesus Thy servant; to Thee be glory forever.

"And concerning the broken bread:

"We give thanks to Thee, our Father, for the life and knowledge which Thou didst make known unto us through Jesus Thy servant; to Thee be glory forever. As this broken bread was scattered on the face of the mountains and gathered together became one, even so may Thy church be gathered together from the ends of the earth into Thy kingdom; for Thine is the glory and power through Jesus Christ forever.

"But let no one eat or drink of your Thanksgiving but they who have been baptized into the name of the Lord, for concerning this the Lord hath said, 'Give not that which is holy unto dogs.' "

It is to be noted that this early eucharistic prayer expresses the gratitude of the *church*. It has none of the individualism of much of our modern worship. All the known accounts of the eucharistic celebration of the early church stress the fact that that celebration was corporate in nature. How then was this original emphasis lost?

Yngve Brilioth says that the first step away from the early practice was taken when the Latin mass was built around the one idea of sacrifice. The Lutheran reformation, in condemning the superstitions which were integral to this view, itself went to the other extreme and laid its entire emphasis on the gift to the individual in communion. In time this position drove out the Eucharist from its place as the chief service of the church. This was as true of Protestantism as of Roman Catholicism. The accent on gratitude which characterized the beginnings of Christian worship in the communion has been reduced to a formal and incidental place. It must be restored to a position of centrality.

"The proper and primitive meaning of the Eucharist is that it is the church's corporate act of praise, culminating in the eucharistic thanksgiving for the objective fact of redemption; and it is this which the church of today must seek to recover," says this Swedish scholar.* When this has been recovered, the church will know once again the radiance of joy which marked the first Christian centuries.

Once that grateful joy overflowed so freely that it gave its quality to the entire communion service. The reason was that the fellowship of believers, thinking of itself as the church, praised God for his redemptive work through the church and for his supreme gift to the body of Christ. Individual thanksgiving for participation in the divine gift must recognize that personal participation is possible only through the church. The church, on its part, must be prepared constantly to acknowledge its precious responsibility to give individuals the opportunity to lose themselves in the church's corporate expression of the thanksgiving.

Protestant individualism has impoverished the observance of the communion and has brought about an undue emphasis on the mystic experience. But even the mystics have begun to forsake their struggle to give the unassisted individual an apprehension of the divine and have turned to the collective

* *Eucharistic Faith and Practice, Evangelical and Catholic,* translated by A. G. Hebert (London: Society for Promoting Christian Knowledge, 1930).

worship of God through the Eucharist. An example is
Evelyn Underhill, one of the most widely known of modern
mystics. She declares that the Eucharist "sums up and expresses the worshiping life of the church. And it is because
every aspect of that response, which the whole created order
makes to its Origin and Lord, finds here its sanction and
expression that the ritual has become the supreme ritual act
of the Christian family, the devotional center of the church's
Godward life; and a deepening sense of its significance one
of the best ways to a fuller participation in that Godward
life." Here God seeks man. Here man responds through the
means provided in the communion. And so "his total dependence on support and nourishment given him from the eternal
is declared and satisfied. The bread of the angels is made the
pilgrim's food . . ."*

This transforming collective thanksgiving stands in the
tradition of the church. It is one with the words of Justin
Martyr (100-165), who addressed a famous "Apology" on
behalf of the Christian community to Emperor Antoninus
Pius. Justin describes how the believer is received into the
Christian fellowship through baptism and the prayers of the
assembled church. Following this comes the communion.
"Then there is presented to the president of the brethren a
loaf and a cup of water and wine and he, after taking them,
offers up praise and glory to the Father of all things, through
the name of the Son and the Holy Ghost; and he gives
thanks at length for these favors of God to us. And when he
has ended the prayers and the thanksgiving (Eucharist) the
whole people present assent with an Amen—the Hebrew

* *The Mystery of Sacrifice* (London: Longmans, Green & Co., 1938),
p.x.

word meaning 'So be it!'—And when the president has given thanks and the whole people have assented, those who are called deacons (ministers) among us receive a portion of the loaf and wine and water, over which the thanksgiving has been made, to [give] each of those who are present, and they take it away to those who are not. And this food is called among us the Eucharist; and no one is allowed to partake of it unless he believes that what we teach is true and has been washed in the laver for the remission of sins and for regeneration and is living as Christ enjoined. For we do not receive these things as common bread or common drink . . ."

In returning to the Eucharist as primarily a corporate act of joyous praise for our redemption through Jesus Christ, the church returns to the high ground from which it started its historic mission across the centuries. It sets the act of thanksgiving in its proper place at the center of worship. It does not abandon penitence or individual gratitude, but it sets both in their proper relation to the jubilant central truth that God was in Christ, reconciling the world unto himself. In so doing the church shines once again with the radiant joy it has lost. It recovers as a gift from God its power to turn the world of complacent evil upside down. Without worry and without laborious contriving it discovers that God is building his kingdom through the incredible overplus which he alone can give to the puny efforts of believing men.

When you awake on the morning of your communion day, give thanks to God particularly that he hath blessed an opportunity of receiving the symbols of pardon, the sacrament of Christ himself, the seed of immortality and the antepast of heaven; and hasten earlier out of your bed. The cock crowing that morning is like the noise that is made by the coming of the bridegroom; and therefore go out to meet him but rise that you may trim your lamp, make a general confession of your sins and be very much humbled in the sense and appreciation of them. Worship Jesus, love him and dedicate thyself to him. Recollect what he hath done for thy soul, what mysteries he hath appointed, by what ministries he conveys himself to thee.

When thou seest the holy man minister, dispute no more, enquire no more, doubt no more, be divided no more; but believe, and behold with the eyes of faith and of the spirit that thou seest Christ's body broken upon the Cross; that thou seest him bleeding for thy sins; that thou feedest upon the food for elect souls; that thou puttest thy mouth to the hole of the rock that was smitten, to the wound in the side of thy Lord, which being pierced streamed forth sacraments and life and holiness and pardon and purity and immortality upon thee. When thou dost receive thy Lord, do thou also receive thy brother into thy heart.

After you have given thanks and finished your private and public devotions, go home. But do not presently forget the solemnity, and sink from the sublimity of devotion and mystery into a secular conversation, like a falling star from brightness into dirt. But what we may do by devotion and solemn religion that day we must do every day by material practice of virtues.

JEREMY TAYLOR in *The Worthy Communicant*

CHAPTER SIX

Blood of the Covenant

This cup is the new covenant in my blood.
— I Corinthians 12:25
And he [Moses] took the book of the covenant,
and read in the audience of the people: and they
said, All that the Lord hath said will we do, and
be obedient. *— Exodus 24:7*

NO HEBREW ever moved out of sight of the mountain on which the Israelites had pledged with Moses their loyalty to the divinity who had delivered them from Egypt. Hebrews believed that on this height Moses had received from the Almighty two stone "tablets of testimony . . . written with the finger of God." But the finger of God did not stop when it had written on the stone. For a long time Israelites believed that it had. The ark in which the stones were carried and the temple in which they had been enshrined had to be destroyed before they would see differently. But when centuries of suffering had driven faith deep into their inward consciousness, Jeremiah came to tell them this better thing:

"Behold, the days come, saith the Lord, that I will make a new covenant with the house of Israel, and with the house of Judah: Not according to the covenant that I made with their fathers, in the day that I took them by the hand to bring them out of the land of Egypt; which my covenant they brake, although I was a husband unto them, saith the Lord: But this shall be the covenant that I will make with the house of Israel; After those days, saith the Lord, I will put my law in their inward parts, and write it in their hearts; and I will be their God, and they shall be my people. And they shall teach no more every man his neighbor, and every man his brother, saying, Know the Lord; for they shall all know me, from the least of them unto the greatest of them, saith the Lord: for I will forgive their iniquity, and I will remember their sin no more" (Jer. 31:31 ff.).

When Jesus stood in the upper room and talked of a new covenant, the disciples recalled these words from the rich heritage of their common history. Like other Jews, they had considered themselves bound by the old covenant. They remembered with pride that while the nation had sometimes failed, multitudes had given their lives rather than violate what they regarded as a solemn compact between God and their people. Memories of apostasies, of dreary years of exile, of the flaming sword of the prophets' wrath, rose before them. But with a glow of assurance they recited to themselves the clearest of all prophecies of the new day they believed was surely coming.

Now Jesus was boldly declaring that he was ready to propose the new covenant which Jeremiah had forecast centuries before. Like the old, this new covenant would also be "written with the finger of God." It too would outlast the centuries. For it men would again gladly give their lives. Instead of being carved on stone it would be inscribed on men's hearts.

Instead of being the treasured possession of a small nation of chosen people it would be acclaimed by a chosen world.

Here was Jesus without hesitation taking upon himself the fulfillment of hopes which had ripened over many generations. He was assuming the responsibility of proclaiming what God would do, of declaring a new basis of relationship between the heavenly Father and his children. This was no legal contract. It was a commitment to eternity. It was to be sealed with his own blood. And it was to be pledged in the Eucharist.

⌊What was—and is—this new covenant which Jesus witnessed with the last full measure of devotion? It was a pledge that through faith the fellowship of the disciples might still possess the indwelling presence of the living Christ. It was the promise that this presence would transform the inner life of the covenanters, bringing the assurance of sins forgiven and the fruits of a changed life. It was also the covenant that out of this would come a revolutionary new order, the kingdom of God. Established institutions would be overturned one after another until all of human society deliberately and willingly adopted as its purpose and constitution the aim of the church to become the family of those who consciously stand in process of redemption by divine grace.⌋ Let us examine this interlocking commitment in more detail.

How could Christ remain with the disciples? Those who met in the upper room expressed no doubt that he would do so. If they had doubts, they were shortly to be resolved. The early church found no need for magic to believe in Christ's continuing presence, though a later, more materialistic age did. To meet the competition of the mystery religions and to speak in terms which the crass barbarians of a savage time could understand, the church tried to pin Christ's presence down to the elements of the Lord's Supper. The bread, it gradually came to teach, was the real body of Christ; the wine, his actual blood. This heresy, installed as the official doctrine of the church by the Fourth Lateran Council in 1215, led to the division of the church at the Reformation. The abuses against which the Reformation was a protest were inevitable because they were inherent in this heretical materialism.

The doctrine of the real presence of Christ in the elements of the Lord's Supper has been debated for centuries. It is unlikely that anything said here will add to human knowledge on the subject or penetrate the institutional encrustations which have grown up around one interpretation or another. But it may not be amiss to point out that in spite of our divisions and apostasies, Christ has carried out his side of the new covenant. If succeeding generations had not had knowledge of the *fact* of his presence, none of the doctrines concerning the meaning of the fact could have lived a very long life. Since this knowledge has not depended upon or been confined to those who maintain that the elements of the Lord's Supper are changed into actual flesh and actual blood, it is reasonable to suppose that such a belief is not necessary to true faith. On the contrary, the history of schism and controversy in the church provides clear evidence that the materialist view is not only dispensable but that it is an error which should be abandoned. What a boon it would be if those who so easily acclaim Augustine would recall his words: "It is a miserable slavery of the soul to take signs for things and to be unable to raise the eye of the mind above the bodily creature to the eternal light."

The alternative to the materialist view of the Lord's Supper is that which is clearly stated in the original New Testament accounts of the observance. Christ's covenant to continue his living presence with his disciples was made with them *as a collectivity*. Even the Roman Catholic Church has never dared to claim that Jesus took one of his disciples aside—it would be Peter, of course—and gave him the communion and commissioned him to administer it in turn to the other disciples. It was of the nature of the new covenant that it was made with the collectivity of the committed friends of Jesus. Individuals were bound by it but only as a consequence of their membership in the church. It might be said, in view of the complexity of human character, that each person was the group in microcosm. But it was with the macrocosm that the compact was made.

In the church the living presence of Christ would find its home. Henceforth this was his body. Here he would reveal himself in the future as he had so often revealed himself in the past. Here his spirit would dominate as it had dominated at the Last Supper. When his friends met and took bread and wine and remembered Christ, making the elements the symbols of his body and blood, he would be in the midst of them. As of old, none who came in faith would be turned away empty. Forgiveness, healing and new power might dependably be found at the table of the Lord in the company of his followers. This was a pledge.

When this happened, the believing covenanters would change. It was of the essence of the covenant that through it the disciples embarked on a strange, alarming but luminous life. "I am in the hands of the Lord as one whose heart he can change and rechange, revive or destroy," Luther once said. Whether Luther was speaking the literal truth concerning himself may be a matter of debate. But his words in this instance might well have been spoken by each of the disciples, except Judas. The extraordinary transformation which came over these timid men after they began to take the new covenant seriously must have amazed themselves. Certainly it astonished the world in which they lived.

It is generally recognized that the experience of fellowship with Christ in the church should involve an ethical as well as a spiritual change in those to whom grace is given. To have one's sins forgiven and to lay aside a burden of guilt and frustration is to find power as well as peace. How much of an outward change this produces depends somewhat on the age and previous behavior of the individual, somewhat on the standards of the culture in which he lives, and a great deal on the vision of his own possibilities and responsibilities which is held before him by that branch of the Christian Church of which he becomes a member. But the promise that change shall occur is firmly rooted in the covenant of the Lord's Supper. From the first Paul made it clear that participation in this observance required a choice. Members were no longer free to attend idolatrous feasts or to engage in devil worship. At the Lord's Supper itself they were to conduct themselves with joy and decorum and to share with the less fortunate members of the community. So the inner presence of Christ in their midst would provide its own witness and justification in the world.

This principle that the covenant which was celebrated in the Lord's Supper involved a two-way obligation was an important factor in the influence of the early church. It should be equally distinctive of the church today. If they, being so few, could hold their disintegrating world together by redeeming the time, how much more should we, being many, feel the responsibility that is on us to do the same.

This brings us to the third aspect of the covenant of the Lord's Supper. It was not enough that the assembly of the covenanters should feel assured of the continuing presence of their Lord or that their inner transformation should lift them above and save them from a dying world. Christ who stood before them at the Last Supper had devoted much of his earthly ministry to preparing the foundation for a new order. It was the revolutionary purpose of this new order to save the world. Christians therefore were not people who were saved out of the world; they were saved in the world. Their high commission was to remain where they were and to build, with a grace and power not their own, the kingdom of God. Thus the covenant was one whose purposes embraced humanity.

It is one of the misfortunes of history that the noble associations of the word covenant have been overlaid by centuries of Protestant as well as Catholic legalism. The limited responsibilities of the typical commercial contract and the sterile associations of religious literalism rise to mind whenever the word is used. Perhaps we can recover something of its beauty and power if we look steadily at what it may have meant to Jesus and to those who surrounded him on that deathless evening in the upper room.

In the Judaism of Jesus' day it was an accepted thing for a religious teacher to gather about himself a group of friends to discuss religion. He and his friends would be known as a *chaburoth*, an association of believers. Usually these groups simply met occasionally to have a meal together. After the meal, which was usually a protracted affair, they would participate in the *kiddush,* the domestic ceremony observed in pious Jewish homes on the eve of the Sabbath or a feast day. Bread and wine were blessed and passed around to all the members of the group. Jesus and his disciples were probably known as such a group. That they remained together more constantly than others and that their discussions went further was in all likelihood not apparent to their contemporaries. It may not have been too clear to all the disciples. They had doubtless met so on other occasions, perhaps many of them.

Then one night Jesus told them that the wickedness he had opposed without compromise was about to take his life. He asked them to carry on his mission of redemption. He declared that God would give him the victory over death and that he would sustain them. When they again came to the bread and wine of the *kiddush,* Jesus asked them to pledge their covenant with him. Taking the familiar elements, he said, "This is my body . . . this is the new covenant in my blood." Henceforth it was impossible for them to meet or to partake of bread and wine, which he had made the symbols of his body and blood, without recalling this pledge. Never again could they eat a meal together without sensing the presence of Jesus.

The story of the two disciples who walked in the country near Jerusalem became a familiar one. All afternoon they had moved along the hilly road, conversing with a stranger. When they confided to him their bewilderment at the sudden debacle of their hopes because of the death of Jesus, the stranger warmly defended the course Jesus had taken. Arriving at a village, they prevailed on their new acquaintance to eat with them at a roadside inn. "When he was at table with them, he took the bread and blessed, and broke it, and gave it to them. And their eyes were opened and they recognized him" (Luke 24:30-31). It was Jesus himself. Ever afterward the expectation that he would appear at a meal of his disciples was kept alive. It was preserved by people who knew that the Stranger of Emmaus never failed to keep his side of the covenant.

If we have wandered from the Christ within the soul, this is our time—this is our place—of return. Again and again, after every failure, we must come back with contrition but without despair. Here is the rendezvous of our fidelity; here our communion once more; here the divine guide with whose will we are henceforth to harmonize our own. This hour is to be hospitable to the holiest messenger of God; to make ready the guest chamber in the upper dwelling of our hearts and to shut out, amid the converse of blessed thoughts, the voices of men and the threatenings of sorrow. Let pure and perfect trust fill all the room; let the Judas-element in our soul rise and quickly pass into the night and the love that remains rest there with freer surrender upon the form of heavenly sanctity.

JAMES MARTINEAU in *Hours of*
Thought on Sacred Things

CHAPTER SEVEN

Broken for You

THE CHRISTIAN faith, which with us too often thins out into an endless flow of words, began in a life filled with deeds. That life ended in a sacrifice of incomparable courage and generosity. It began again in the deed by which God gave Christ the victory over death. It continued in the fellowship which transformed a decadent society by the enduring strength of the Christian Church. In the church the presence of the living Christ provided sustaining power to those who believed in him and kept his commandments. In the Lord's Supper this continuing presence was recognized and honored.

All true worship and therefore all honest observance of the Lord's Supper must contain the element of sacrifice. The term comes from two words—*sacrum faciens*—meaning the act by which one consecrates something to God. By partaking in faith of the symbols of Christ's sacrifice, we offer ourselves to God. We identify our own lives with his life. We acknowledge that the principle which led Jesus Christ to the cross should rule our own decisions. We seek strength to follow where he leads. Instead of attempting to consecrate bread and wine by pretending to add to them a magical surcharge they would not have unless we intervened to bring it down on them, we recognize that in the upper room and on Calvary

Jesus consecrated these elements "far above our poor power to add or detract."

But Jesus did not sacrifice *me*. He did not lay my faith, my love, my daily endeavor, my hopes and fears, my penitent tears, at the feet of God. Only I can do that. In the Lord's Supper I can do it in fellowship with the living Christ and with his church.

The early Christians were jubilantly aware that they had had something extraordinarily precious done for them. This they had not earned or deserved. No merit they possessed or could acquire could repay God for what he had done for them. Like other Jews, they had felt themselves under a historic constraint of gratitude to God for his deliverance of the people of Israel from slavery in Egypt. More than most of their countrymen, the disciples were thankful for the progressive revelation of the will and purpose of God as unfolded by the long succession of prophets. They were heirs of the prophetic tradition. Now God had given them Jesus Christ. Jesus had shared their sufferings. He had revealed the divine possibilities of their common life and had thus uncovered the horror of missing the mark and negating those possibilities. Their response was overwhelming appreciation for an unspeakable blessing which had been conveyed to them—of all people—without their having done anything to deserve it.

The disciples of Jesus not only did not claim the beneficence of God as a right; they recognized that their sins had had a direct bearing on the crucifixion of their Lord. They never sat down to the communion without recalling that it was one of their own number who betrayed Jesus for thirty pieces of silver. It is impossible to read the New Testament language concerning Judas without sensing in its violence the guilt which all the disciples felt over his treachery. After all, they had not been far from such betrayal themselves. All of them had deserted Jesus on the night of his arrest. Some had openly denied knowing him. The rest had crept silently away, acting the same lie. None had done anything about which he might justly develop the slightest sense of superiority over the others.

When they took the bread of the Eucharist, therefore, and heard the words, "broken for you," they fully recognized the sacrifice of Jesus for what it was: the free outreach of God to sinners who had no mortgage on his beneficence and who could not acquire such a claim. It was clearly a gift of the grace of God. Out of the goodness of his heart, God had sent his Son that whosoever believed on him might not perish but live forever. God shared in the sacrifice of the cross. Those who stood helplessly on Golgotha while Jesus died under the frightful torture of the nails, the spears and the pitiless sun were aware that they were looking on the agony of God as well as the sacrifice of Christ. And it was *for them* that divinity travailed.

At the Last Supper in the upper room the disciples were at last attempting to grasp the meaning of the sacrifice Jesus seemed determined to make. Now the Master was confronting them with a fact that they had sought throughout the years of their association with him to evade. They could escape no longer. They must face reality.

What was Jesus attempting to accomplish through the sacrifice symbolized in the Eucharist? The question presumes that he could have saved his life had he chosen to do so. This might have been achieved in two ways. He might have modified his message to make it more acceptable to those who were antagonized by anything that menaced the old order. Or he might have continued as before but giving encouragement to those who wanted to organize force for his protection and for the overthrow of the corrupt established system. What minister of the gospel does not recognize the reality of the first temptation? And what historian does not acknowledge the feasibility of the second? The country was ripe for revolt and did repeatedly attempt before and after Jesus' death to throw off the Roman yoke.

But the Nazarene chose neither of these alternatives. He continued to teach a revolutionary doctrine which he knew would cause his enemies to bring about his death, yet he did nothing to avert this fate. When the crisis came, he steadfastly set his face toward Jerusalem and all that awaited him there. The reason must have been that he believed his death would continue to serve the purposes to which he had given his life. Indeed, it seems that he became convinced that under the circumstances his death was necessary to the fulfillment of his mission. Why this was so was the primary question that filled the minds of the disciples in the upper room.

Nobody can fully answer the question that haunted the disciples. Even after twenty centuries the replies which the church has given seem pallid and weak in the face of the stark terror and tragedy of the cross. But as long as humanity cannot tear itself away from the foot of that cross or abandon the symbol of his sacrifice which Jesus provided in the holy communion, men and women of faith must attempt to understand what they mean. We must do so knowing that even when we have done our reverent best, we can only penetrate the fringes of the mystery. The ultimate answers to both sin and redemption lie at the center.

Jesus found the meaning of sacrifice in the nature of God. Throughout his ministry he had taught that God is the compassionate Father of the human family. His children find their highest destiny when they love one another and witness to the goodness of God. But since they are endowed with freedom, which is integral to their nature as volitional beings, they are free to choose evil as well as good. This we all do, and some of us cling to evil with ingenuity and extraordinary persistence. In a moral universe, the choice of evil brings suffering and death. Since men are members of one human family, the good suffer with the wrongdoers for the evil that is done. They must nevertheless persist in their effort to choose good rather than evil and to be reconciled to God, who is always ready to forgive transgressors.

It is the Christian belief that the power of God is greater even than death. We hold this view because Jesus, when he was confronted with the alternative of compromise or death on the cross, chose the cross. The form in which the issue presented itself to him that night in the upper room may have been something like this: He had witnessed to the love of God. Now the forces of evil, refusing to repent, sought his life. What should he do? He had taught that evil is overcome with good. Should he now, to save his own life, attempt to overcome evil with evil? That is what he would be doing if he began to "fight fire with fire." Having taught that God is love, Jesus refused to admit that not love but hatred must be his ultimate reliance.

But if his enemies killed him, would not that represent the triumph of evil? It would unless God could surmount death. Jesus believed that God could and would. He was prepared to put his faith to the test. If the test failed, the disillusionment would be no greater than if he himself abandoned his faith to save his life. If it succeeded, the centuries would see to it that so precious a fact would live and become the cornerstone of the kingdom of God on earth. Jesus made his sacrifice in faith. God did not let him down.

Against this view of the meaning of his sacrifice the Christian Church itself has fought almost as vigorously as did the disciples. Even yet large sections prefer to hold that on the cross Jesus was propitiating an angry God who demanded either his Son's death or the destruction of the rest of his impenitent family of children. The official doctrine of the Roman Catholic and Eastern churches is that God's implacable wrath continues, and is contained only because of the repeated offering in the mass of the actual body and blood of his ever dying Son. Many Protestants also accept this view, substituting the blood atonement for the mass. All who do so represent God as an ogre and the scene on Calvary as a frightful market transaction in the most precious blood that was ever shed. The alternative is to admit that Jesus gave his life rather than abandon his faith in God's love and power.

One reason why many Christians object to keeping the events of the close of Jesus' ministry in the realm of history is the apparent failure of Jesus' sacrifice. Pilate and Caiaphas and the other evil men who did him to death died in their sins. So far as anybody could see, their power was unshaken by the events of Calvary. The mob might be restive for a while, but it would forget. The systems of power which these leaders represented would crumble, but others would rise to take their place. What then was the use of a sacrifice which made so little immediate impression? A legend even grew up that in later years Pilate completely forgot the strange

Galilean whose cause he had betrayed in history's most in-famous judicial murder. A church that would foster such a legend was one which was attempting to justify the seeming futility of Jesus' sacrifice.

But it missed the point. The disciples did not forget. The body which was so brutally broken on the cross was broken for them. Jesus did not say at the Last Supper that his body was broken for Pilate or Caiaphas. They were not outside the hope of redemption, it was true, provided they repented and believed. But Jesus placed his confidence in the church. In time the seekers after power would see, as their kind always does, where their own advantage lay when the influence of the church grew. But now and always it was the church to which the light was entrusted.

The flaming faith of the disciples under the new covenant was the courage of men whose fear of death was gone. Since all fear ultimately is an aspect of the fear of death, so all courage is in essence the affirmation of life. Freed from the source of fear, the disciples triumphantly affirmed the reality of the life that was in Christ Jesus. They counted it all joy to share in his sacrifice, even the suffering of the cross, because through it they had learned that the God Jesus worshiped can conquer even death and that he does so still for those who believe in his love and trust his good faith.

To recapitulate the items adduced in favor of the ancient order of breaking bread, it was shown, as we apprehended:

1. That there is a divinely instituted order of Christian worship in Christian assemblies.

2. That this order of worship is uniformly the same.

3. That the nature and design of the breaking of bread are such as to make it an essential part of Christian worship in Christian assemblies.

4. That the first church set in order in Jerusalem continued as steadfastly in the breaking of bread as in any other act of social worship or edification.

5. That the disciples statedly met on the first day of the week primarily and emphatically for this purpose.

6. That the apostle [Paul] declared it was the design or the primary object of the church to assemble in one place for this purpose and so commanded it to the churches he had set in order.

7. That there is no law, rule, reason or authority for the present manner of observing this institute quarterly, semi-annually or at any other time than weekly.

ALEXANDER CAMPBELL in *The Christian Baptist*, August 1, 1825

CHAPTER EIGHT

This Is My Body

The bread which we break, is it not a participation in the body of Christ? Because there is one loaf, we who are many are one body, for we all partake of the same loaf.
— *I Corinthians 10:16-17*

IN THE upper room Jesus was talking. One of the words he used was "you." He used it in the collective sense. Jesus addressed the disciples as a group. The bread, he said, was a symbol of their unity. Like grains of wheat gathered from scattered places, ground into flour, kneaded into dough and baked as bread, they had merged their identities and become one. Jesus, in surrendering his body to death, henceforth would live in them. The breaking of bread was therefore a compact between himself and the Christian community. The disciples in partaking of this bread were affirming their unity with him and with each other in the church. For the relationship which obtained between Jesus and his disciples would henceforth hold between him and his church.

Nothing stands out with more unmistakable clarity than the concern of the early church to maintain its integrity and its solidarity. The sacraments of baptism and the Lord's Sup-

per were both pledges to that end. Baptism was recognized
as marking the believer's entry into the unity of the church.
It was an affirmation that he had died to his former isolated
life and had now been raised up by grace to live the life of
the community of faith. The observance of the Lord's Supper
was always understood as a pledge on the part of the participant to live in and to maintain the solidarity of the Christian fellowship. No member was permitted to share in the
communion who had broken that fellowship by hatred or
quarreling. The extraordinary measures which were taken to
reconcile members who had differences were the heroic efforts
of the Christian body to preserve its integrity. Unreconciled
persons were plainly told that they had no place at the table
of the Lord, not merely because they offended against themselves and each other by strife, but basically because they had
sinned against Christ by dividing his body.

The relation between this rigorous standard of unity and
the Lord's Supper is shown in the New Testament and in
the writings of the earliest church fathers. The words of Paul
and John in this connection are well known. They clearly
reveal the passion for unity which was from the beginning
central in the thought of the church. They also show that this
passion was something very much more than the necessity
which rests on an institution to maintain its health and vigor.
This church was one because Christ is undivided. It jealously
guards its integrity because only through that can it bear true
witness to the nature of its Lord. Through him alone is there
hope that the divided family of God may one day be reunited.
By partaking in symbol of his body Christians proclaim the
essential unity of his church and point the way to the reconciliation of men with each other and with God. "For just as

the body is one and has many members, and all the members of the body, though many, are one body, so it is with Christ. ... Now you are the body of Christ and individually members of it" (I Cor. 12:12,27).

Ignatius, the earliest of the church fathers, noted this unitive meaning of the communion. He wrote to the Ephesians urging "that ye all by name come together in common in the faith and in Jesus Christ . . . breaking the same bread, which is the medicine of immortality." He urged the appointment of bishops or elders to supervise its observance in the interest of unity. He speaks of the Eucharist as the "one flesh of our Lord and one cup for union with his blood." A little later Clement of Rome wrote that "we ought to do all things in order, whatsoever the Lord has commanded us to perform at stated times: the oblations and liturgies to be celebrated and that they should not take place at random or disorderly but at definite times and hours." It may be well to recall that the emphasis on order was at first an attempt to strengthen the unity of the church by making its observances acceptable to the majority of its members. Later, it became a divisive accent on protocol.

In the *Teaching of the Apostles* (100 A. D.) this irenic counsel is given: "On the day of the Lord, being assembled together, break bread and give thanks, after confession of your trespasses, that your sacrifice may be pure. And let no one who has a dispute with his companion come with you until they are reconciled, that our sacrifice may not be defiled." A communion prayer in the same document contains these words: "Remember, Lord, thy church to deliver it from all evil and to perfect it in thy love and gather it together from the four winds, the sanctified, unto thy kingdom which

thou hast prepared for it; for thine is the power and the glory
forever. Come, Grace, and pass this world away. Hosanna
to the God of David. If anyone is holy, let him come. If anyone is not, let him repent. Maranatha. Amen. But allow the
prophets to give thanks as much as they will!" Christian unity
was not inconsistent with the liberty that is in Christ.

One of the reasons for the complacency with which Christians commonly tolerate the divisions of the church is that we
have never considered carefully the corporate nature of the
act of worship which is the Lord's Supper. Both Catholic
and Protestant have thought of it as primarily the act of the
individual Christian. This is a mistake. The communion is
primarily between Christ and the church. Only as a member
of the church, the body of Christ, can any of us share in the
Lord's Supper. We fail indeed to "discern the Lord's body,"
as did those against whose blindness Paul inveighed, if we do
not see that our individual blessing is possible only because
we are united with other souls in the Church of Christ. This
need not be interpreted narrowly as requiring membership
in a particular denomination. But it does require a conscious
repentance for sin, a renunciation with the help of God of
secularism and separatism, and an entry into the joyous unity
of the Christian community.

Here it becomes necessary to discuss what is called "closed
communion." In general this practice represents an attempt
on the part of ministers or others who presume to act on
behalf of the church to decide who shall be excluded from
the Lord's Supper. Sometimes the excluding has been done
by congregational officers who decline to permit persons
known to be living in hatred or other sin to commune until
they repent. Where every effort has been made without suc-

cess to bring the sinner to repentance, it is impossible to deny that the congregation has this right and, indeed, this obligation. Flagrant and persistent violation of the spiritual basis of the Christian fellowship cannot be tolerated indefinitely without the destruction and demoralization of that fellowship.

But the decision to exclude a person from communion is a grave one. It is not to be taken lightly but in the fear of God. The act of communion, if sincerely entered into, is itself a request for forgiveness and a declaration of repentance. Only the most conclusive evidence of lack of good faith justifies a ban on participation in the communion by one who affirms his desire to partake of it. For it is not *our* feast—it is the *Lord's* Supper. And we are not the Lord.

Regrettably, the reason for the practice of closed communion is often much more trivial. In some denominations it is the custom to bar from communion all persons who are not members of that denomination. It is sometimes not denied that these persons may be Christians, but they are held to be Christians of lesser stature and a lower level because they are not members of a particular group. This is an untenable position and unworthy of disciples of Christ. In other cases it is declared that persons who do not subscribe to the particular views represented by a denomination are not Christians, even though they believe they are and live lives not noticeably different from those of other Christians. In both cases some individual or group, either by statute or by tradition, constitute themselves a tribunal to decide what they have no right to decide. They judge, forgetting that they will be judged. They divide the body of Christ.

The following true incident will illustrate the point. Into a southern church which practices closed communion came a minister of the northern branch of the same denomination. The church had been divided by the tensions leading to the Civil War. Now, years later, the wounds of the war were healing and the two denominations were drawing together. The northern minister had been invited to preach and the service had progressed beyond the sermon to the Lord's Supper. The deacons passed among the congregation with the bread and wine.

A layman noticed that everybody was served but the minister, although by courtesy he was usually served first. He rose to ask the reason. The presiding officer rather hesitantly said that it was the tradition of the church to serve only members of its own denomination. The layman promptly answered: "If this good man, this minister of the gospel whose sermon has opened the Scriptures to us this morning, is barred from taking communion in this church, I also have no right to partake." He then poured his wine on the floor and dropped his bread and stepped on it. The congregation was appalled at his act, but when its meaning became clear to them they insisted on his remaining a member and discontinued the practice of closed communion.

This layman's startling deed was not half so shocking as the practice against which it was a protest. His spontaneous rejection of symbols of the unity of the church which had lost their meaning was no desecration. It was a holy act. He was taking the most direct way immediately available to affirm the solidarity of the church which included both himself and the minister. He was protesting forcefully against the real desecration of the unity of the body of Christ which is represented in the practice of closed communion. Something of the same quality of protest is found in the rejection by the Society of Friends of all observance of the Lord's Supper. They refuse to partake of a symbol of unity whose perversion by the church has so often made it both the occasion and the emblem of division and strife.

Another reason given for excluding from the Lord's Supper members of other churches depends upon a certain conception of the ministry. According to this view, church membership is divided into two classes. Bishops and other clergymen are believed to possess a special holiness because they have been set aside by the laying on of hands of men who themselves have been ordained in this manner. This succession is held to go back in unbroken line to the twelve apostles, and to endow a man so consecrated with a sanctity not accessible to ordinary members of the church. These constitute another and lower class of Christians. Only the clergy can properly administer the Lord's Supper, it is supposed. Therefore only those persons are communing members of the church who have received the emblems of the Lord's Supper from ministers belonging to the apostolic succession.

This theory depends upon an interpretation of what happened in the upper room which cannot be sustained by a study of the documents. It is true that Jesus was consecrating his disciples as ministers, but it is not true that they were set above all other members of the body of Christ. These others too were ministers. Under the headship of Christ his body has no room in it for caste or class. It was the church which became the body of Christ, not a hierarchy. Nothing in Jesus' entire ministry, in his characteristic attitudes or in the authentic records of the early church gives ground for believing that he intended to set up at the Lord's Supper a principle of division which would separate Christians into first- and second-class followers. By the same token, nothing justifies the practice of barring some Christians from the communion because they have not been received into the church by ministers who have been set aside by this principle. Jesus said, "You are my disciples," not, "You are my overlords." He said, "This is my body," not, "These are my bodies." He provided in the symbol of the bread a simple example of unity created out of diversity which must certainly have been intended to teach the church constantly to guard its solidarity. Paul understood it that way. "The bread which we break, is it not a participation in the body of Christ? Because there is one loaf, we who are many are one body, for we all partake of the same loaf." The writer of the Gospel of John saw no principle of hierarchy in the church. "I do not pray for these only [Jesus had been talking about the twelve disciples], but also for those who are to believe in me through their word, that they may all be one; even as thou, Father, art in me, and I in thee, that they also may be in us, so that the world may believe that thou hast sent me. The glory which thou hast given me I have given to them, that they may be one even as we are one, I in them and thou in me, that they may become perfectly one, so that the world may know that thou hast sent me and hast loved them even as thou hast loved me" (John 17:20-23). Such language indicates that even as late as the second generation after Christ, when these words were probably written, the doctrine of apostolic succession as a basis for discriminating among Christians at communion was unheard of.

The reason for this unity must not be forgotten. It was "that the world may believe that thou hast sent me." Jesus constantly declared that he had a divine commission but he recognized that his claim would not be believed unless his followers bore a credible witness to it. Otherwise he could be regarded as just another impostor whose sweeping pretensions were not accompanied by commensurate achievement. How much we have done to make a sectarian, a pretender, a mountebank out of Christ! Dare we ever partake of the bread of his body in the communion without asking his forgiveness?

Fortunately the church is beginning to bring forth fruits appropriate to repentance. World Communion Sunday is one such blessed achievement. On the first Sunday in October churches in all lands call their members together in this significant observance. On that day at least, when the people of every country break bread they can truly say, "This is my body." May the promise contained in that holy day soon be fulfilled for all churches and throughout the year! For, "because there is one loaf, we who are many are one body, for we all partake of the same loaf."

Here God the supernatural seeks man by natural vehicles and lowly ways, and man, the creature of the borderland, makes his small response by the same means: and in these homely and sacred acts of fraction and communion by which the church has continuously experienced the presence of her Master, his total dependence on support and nourishment given him from the eternal is declared and satisfied. The bread of the angels is made the pilgrim's food, under the humble accidents of the bread and wine, and thus man learns to recognize the constant, mysterious intermingling, yet utter distinctness, of his natural and supernatural life.

EVELYN UNDERHILL in *The Mystery of Sacrifice* (London, Longmans, Green & Company, 1938), page x

CHAPTER NINE

By Whom We Are Reconciled

*For if while we were enemies we were reconciled
to God by the death of his Son, much more, now
that we are reconciled, shall we be saved by his
life. Not only so, but we also rejoice in God through
our Lord Jesus Christ, through whom we have now
received our reconciliation. — Romans 5:10-11*

*For this is my blood of the covenant, which is
poured out for many for the forgiveness of sins.*
— Matthew 26:28

*The bread which I shall give for the life of the
world is my flesh.* *— John 6:51*

JESUS CHRIST is living today. His presence is a reality to
men and women of faith. It is particularly realized when we
who constitute the church partake of the symbols of Christ's
life in the holy communion. Then we know that through his
mercy we who are sinners have been reconciled to God. Our
participation in the communion celebrates that reconciliation.

Our share in the Lord's Supper will be enriched if we
consider the meaning of reconciliation in relation to our act.
We should do this because we declare, as we partake of the

71

communion, that we who were estranged from our heavenly
Father and aliens to the Christian community are now united
by bonds of love with Christ and his church. We hail the
miracle of redemption. We proclaim our at-one-ment with
our Creator and with the fellowship of those who love and
serve the Lord. We not only obey but "we also rejoice in
God," as Paul says, "through our Lord Jesus Christ, through
whom we have now received our reconciliation."

But we do more than celebrate the fact of our own reconciliation in the Lord's Supper. We bear witness to our faith
that the redemptive process which brings this blessed result
still continues. It is an active principle of present life as well
as the germinal element in past history. God is still in the
living Christ, reconciling the world unto himself. In the
Eucharist we re-enact the cardinal principle of reconciliation,
which is that Christ, through his life, teaching, sufferings and
death, saves men from sin and destruction by bringing them
to a knowledge of God, whom to know is life eternal.

How do the symbols of the body and blood of Christ reach
beyond Christ and bear witness to the nature of God? This
question carries us back to the upper room. But we cannot
reach that holy place without passing Golgotha. Christ is
hanging there on the lonely hill, dying between two thieves,
because he refused to abandon his faith that God is truly
our Father and that he is able to overcome evil, even the evil
of death, by good. Remembering this, we turn backward
another day and sit with the disciples in the upper room.
Now we see, as in Georgia O'Keeffe's painting, a picture
framed by the arms of the cross. Patiently Christ is making
one more attempt to explain what is about to happen.

These things must be, Jesus says. Why? Because God is

like that. The life I have lived has shown you the Father. My words have shown you the Father. Now my dying also will show you the Father. It will reveal God riven by agony, overshadowed by death, forsaken and reviled. It will disclose how far love will go. You will see love storm the gates of death itself and plant its flag on the ultimate pinnacle of man's frustration. And God's purpose in it all is your redemption. He asks nothing more in satisfaction for your sin, whose magnitude is measured by his suffering, than that you repent and believe. Take then these elements of my life as an affirmation that you turn away from your evil ways and have faith in me as God's Son and in my Father in whose likeness I live and die.

This theory is known, not too happily, as the moral view of the atonement. It is the only view of the atonement that is consistent with the note of joyous thanksgiving which dominated the observance of the Lord's Supper in the early church. It is profoundly religious. It represents God, whose law is the foundation of the moral order, acting as a moral being. It is compatible with the nature of the Creator as the divine Father. "For God so loved the world that he gave his only Son, that whoever believes in him should not perish but have eternal life." It has power to unlock in the nature of man capacities for faith and service, for love and loyalty, which no other conviction can release. And it naturally fits the teachings and the conduct of Jesus throughout his life into the grand design of the ultimate union of the family of God.

This point is stressed because it is now necessary to consider two other views of reconciliation. The first has had less influence than the second. This is the view originally promulgated by Grotius (1583-1645), the Dutchman who was

the father of international law. It is known as the govern-
mental theory. It is the position that whenever a law is vio-
lated, somebody must be punished, else the relations of citizens
within the community will lapse into disorder and anarchy.
The death of Jesus Christ, said Grotius, was God's punishment for the sin of the race. It was necessary that somebody
should be punished as a warning to men. Jesus' death satisfied
the demands of law and made unnecessary the divine punishment of men for their own sins.

This view is untenable because it violates both love and
justice. It is true that the innocent suffer for the sins of the
guilty, but they suffer *with* the wrongdoer, not *instead of* him,
and they do it not by arbitrary fiat but because men are
members of one family. To picture God as inflicting the cross
on his sinless Son simply as a device of celestial administration is to place him on a lower level than even earthly gov-
ernors, who at least try to approximate justice by holding each
man responsible for his conduct. Western law long ago rose
above the conception of substitutionary punishment Grotius
describes. He overlooks entirely the supreme fact that it is
God's nature not only to rule but also to love, his activity as a
sovereign being qualified by and dependent upon his father-
hood.

We now come to the second and historically more influ-
ential theory of the atonement, one held by both Roman
Catholic and Calvinistic theologians. As outlined by Anselm
(1034-1109), the father of Scholasticism, it declared that
only a God-man could render to God the satisfaction God
demanded if he were to forgive man's sin and so make redemption possible. As a man Jesus did his duty, which was
required of him as a man, and so had no merit to spare. But

in voluntarily taking upon himself the sufferings of death, which he was not required to do, Jesus created a reservoir of merit upon which sinful men can draw and so satisfy an implacable God.

Anselm believed that Jesus dies again each time the Eucharist is celebrated, since the elements are his living body and blood, and so the store of merit is increased. God therefore is further propitiated each time the Eucharist is served. He is appeased still more whenever a saint imitates Christ. The church is God's agent for building up the store of merit and for administering it through its penitential system.

Thus Anselm's view of the atonement becomes the basis for the whole vast machinery of Roman Catholicism. In particular, it is the bulwark of clericalism, since only the priesthood can work the miracle of creating Christ and putting him to death in the mass. It led to the declaration by the Council of Trent in 1545 : "This sacrament no one can effect, unless a priest who has been duly ordained, according to the keys of the church which Jesus Christ himself granted to the apostles and their successors."

Calvin (1509-64) held the same view in essence, although he did not accept the elaborations of it which made the Roman Catholic Church the necessary administrator of the penitential system. This French lawyer also taught that sin has utterly alienated man from God and that Christ saves men by vicariously enduring the punishment intended for them by a wrathful deity. Jesus, he wrote, "bore the weight of the divine anger, was smitten and afflicted, and experienced all the signs of an angry and avenging God," including the descent into hell. The primary characteristic of the sovereign God is justice, Calvin believed. Such a God demands punishment commensurate with the sin committed. God can forgive the guilty only because his Son has suffered the just penalty for sin. Even then he can forgive only those whom he has elected for redemption, the rest being hopelessly damned. In the Lord's Supper, therefore, we celebrate the fact that God has been propitiated, that our sin has been expiated, that the law has been satisfied, that God's wrath has vented itself on his Son instead of on us, that reparation has been made.

What happens to this legalism when it is set alongside the teachings of Jesus? Measure it for example by the parable of the Prodigal Son. Was the father in this story, which contains Jesus Christ's description of the process leading to reconciliation, an "angry and avenging" parent? Did he demand the death of his elder son in satisfaction for the great wrong which the younger had committed? Did he consent to forgive only after he was reminded by the administrator of his estate that the older had faithfully served him and had therefore accumulated a store of merit sufficient for both? Such questions answer themselves. The parable would have been different from beginning to end if Jesus had had any such conception of God as that held by Anselm or Calvin.

How the Lord's Supper would have differed from what the New Testament tells us it originally was if Christ had had in mind their conception of his Father! Propitiation, appeasement, conciliation, reparation—these ideas find not the slightest foundation in any of the five New Testament accounts of the Eucharist. When did Jesus ever talk about giving God "satisfaction" for sin? When did he use the word "expiation"? When did he ever describe God as a ruler whose only concern was order instead of a Father whose passion is redemption? When did he picture the Creator as an absentee landlord who turned over the administration of his affairs to underlings to whom he entrusted his own divine powers?

If Jesus had had this idea of atonement, Paul's account of the institution of the Lord's Supper might read something like this: "I received from the Lord what I also delivered to you, that the Lord Jesus on the night when he was betrayed took bread, and when he had given thanks, he broke it, and said, 'This is my body which is broken in order that God, who can never forgive you otherwise, will vent his wrath on me. Do this in remembrance of me, who love you, but do not forget the Almighty, who is an angry and avenging God.' In the same way also the cup, after supper, saying, 'This cup is the new convenant in my blood, for God must be satisfied, and only my death can restrain his wrath. Do this, as often as you drink it, in remembrance of me. For as often as you eat this bread and drink the cup, you proclaim the Lord's death until he comes.' " And Anselm might continue: "You also add to the credit side of the divine ledger a certain surplus of merit on which you or another can draw to propitiate God, who never forgets and who will throw you into eternal bankruptcy in hell if your account runs short by a penny. *law* So keep on the right side of the church which has been appointed to administer the merit bank."

Such a paraphrase, of course, is little short of blasphemous. But the blasphemy lies not in the words, but in the conception of God which requires such an outrageous distortion of the plain language of the Scriptures if it is to be held with consistency. Certainly no such view can stand in the clear light which shines from the New Testament record, to which we are well advised to turn when we bear our necessary wit-

ness in the Eucharist to the wonder and majesty of the reconciliation with God through Christ.

These three are the principal explanations of what we
mean when, in the Lord's Supper, we proclaim Christ as the
reconciler. Others have been offered, but they are variants
of these three. Sometimes it has been said that Jesus Christ
suffered simply because it was predicted in the Old Testament that he would do so. On the basis of the figurative
language of such passages as Mark 10:45 ("For the Son of
man also came not to be served but to serve, and to give his
life a ransom for many") it is said that Jesus' life was the
purchase price paid for the freeing of enslaved men. From
this symbolically true statement it was only a step to the
superstition, widely held in the Roman Catholic Church before Anselm, that the ransom was paid by God to the devil.
Gregory of Nyssa held the unedifying theory that man's
deliverance was due to God's ability to hoodwink Satan, who
was deceived by Jesus' humanity until the resurrection, after
which it was too late for Satan to destroy Christ. Out of this
grew such shocking metaphors as Gregory the Great's "Our
Lord's humanity was the bait placed on the hook of his
divinity," and Peter Lombard's "The cross is a mousetrap
baited by Jesus' blood."

More modern thought emphasizes the social aspect of the
atonement. In his book *Atonement and Personality*,* R. C.
Moberly says that "the primary object of the death of Christ
is the creation of a community in which the bond of union is
the acceptance of his principle of self-sacrificing love." Ritschl
maintained that the purpose of God is not primarily the salvation of souls but their union in a redeemed society—the

* New York: Longmans, Green & Co., 1901.

kingdom of God. The experience of divine forgiveness, he held, is possible only to those men who make Christ's wider social purpose their own. Concerning both these representative positions it can be said that they exhibit the advantages and share the weaknesses of all collectivism. They place the individual personality in a secondary position in order to serve individual interests more perfectly, and end up by destroying that which they seek to serve if they go too far. But they rightly emphasize the importance of always thinking of the role of the church in reconciliation and the necessity that redeemed individuals shall associate themselves together for the worship of the Lord and for doing his redeeming work in the world.

The Christian Church has given more thought to the atonement than to any other doctrine for the very good reason that reconciliation is the heart of our faith. Whatever the church has thought has depended in the last analysis on its idea of the nature of God. His purpose cannot be inconsistent with his nature. We believe we see his nature in his Son Jesus Christ. As we sit at the communion table with him, no conception can mean more than the faith that "God was in Christ reconciling the world to himself." That faith we appropriate for ourselves and for our generation when we assemble with other Christians and partake believingly of the Lord's Supper, remembering him who is the author and finisher of our faith, even Jesus Christ.

Accept, O Lord our God, this heartfelt supplication which we thine unworthy servants make before thee, that thou, forgiving us all our offenses, wouldst remember all our enemies which hate and evilly entreat us: reward them not after their works, but turn thou such among them as believe not unto the right faith and true worshipping of thee, and such as yet believe that they may forsake evil and do good. Mercifully deliver thy holy Church from all the evils which beset her, preserve her from all heresy and schism, and establish her in peace and concord. Preserve our motherland from the power of the ungodly and from evil men. Grant unto us all that, being speedily reconciled, we may lead a quiet and peaceable life in all godliness and honesty, and may have brotherly love one towards another in thy Christ.

> From a prayer used at the daily celebration of the Eucharist in all the Russian Orthodox churches of the emigration

CHAPTER TEN

Until He Comes

For as often as you eat this bread and drink the
cup, you proclaim the Lord's death until he comes.
— I Corinthians 11:26

EVERY OBSERVANCE of the Lord's Supper makes some
kind of assumption about immortality. Whether so intended
or not, each such act fosters one point of view or another
about the life to come. The observance which simply memo-
rializes the fact that Jesus once lived assumes the survival
of man's influence for good or evil. The rite which hails
the persistence of Christ's spirit in his church declares that
a man may also live on after his death in the institutions and
associations to which he has given himself. The celebration
which recognizes Christ's presence at or in the Lord's Supper ✓
proclaims that in some sense his personality survives, and if
Jesus lives, then all who seek to follow him must accept
immortality as a fact of supreme importance.

Since every observance of the Eucharist makes some kind
of assumption about immortality, it is necessary that these
assumptions be examined. If we teach through these assumptions, we need to be concerned that what we teach is true.
We should see to it that the teaching is done openly and with

81

an appropriate sense of responsibility. Furthermore, we should exercise care that what our observance of the Lord's Supper teaches about immortality is recognized to stand along with other meanings of the rite, receiving as much attention as is its due, but no more.

Because Christians celebrate the resurrection of Christ on the first day of every week, any Sunday is an appropriate time for the church to consider the teaching of the Eucharist concerning the future of man's soul. But pre-eminent among all these occasions is Easter. On that day we declare in the Lord's Supper as well as in sermon and music that Christian hope is forever bright, Christian confidence is eternally renewed, Christian love is perpetually deepened, because God brought Christ back from the dead. Through colorful ritual and song and through the ancient story we give grateful expression to the joy which the faithful of all the centuries since the resurrection have found in the living presence of the Lord.

Let there be no mistake about the assumption underlying our observance of the Lord's Supper. Let there be no confusion about what we intend to teach. Let there be no laxity in making that teaching as clear as the sun on Easter hills. We assume personal immortality. We teach what Kant described as "the indefinitely prolonged existence and personality of one and the same rational being." This is not the same thing as the persistence of influence, although one is not required to deny that personality does extend itself in that way also. It is not "corporate immortality," although that form of continuity undoubtedly exists and makes its identifiable mark on history. It is not even the continuing life of God, into whose vast sea of being some would like to believe man sinks, losing his identity and manifesting himself thereafter if at all only as a transient ripple or an ephemeral wave on the surface of the great deep. It is the immortality of the person as a person.

It is highly important that Christians think clearly about immortality, particularly in their observance of the Eucharist. At the Last Supper, Jesus stood in the shadow of death. He knew, even if those who were with him did not, that the cross was already waiting. He did not fear it, but he desired more than anything else that his disciples should share his conviction that the power and love of God could triumph over death itself. That conviction was a far cry from the sentimentalism of much modern thought about the life to come. A good deal of bad theology is concealed within the cadence of lines like those by George Eliot which are too often repeated in church assemblies:

> O may I join the choir invisible
> Of those immortal dead who live again
> In minds made better by their presence; live
> In pulses stirred to generosity,
> In deeds of daring rectitude, in scorn
> For miserable aims that end with self,
> In thoughts sublime that pierce the night like stars,
> And with their mild persistence urge man's search
> To vaster issues.

Here George Eliot confines immortality to the persistence of influence. But the only survival that is worthy of the name is the survival of personality. The materialist denies such survival, declaring that it is impossible because life depends upon the body. He holds that when man's physical organism ceases to exist, his body and brain dissolve and all that makes

him a man dies. But he stands silent before the fact that man
can always distinguish himself from his body, can often rise
above its clamant demands, can control it through his will.
He cannot explain how man is conscious of his identity and
continues as a living person even though his body changes
completely every seven years. He has no answer to the questions raised by man's capacity to transcend his physical limitations and to "think God's thoughts after him" as he enters
into the mysteries of the universe.

The naturalist also fails when he tries to deny immortality
because in his view man is inescapably trapped in the endless
mutations of nature. Try as he will, he cannot confine this
creature within his creaturely cycles of evolution and dissolu-
tion. Man is a tenant of a physical organism, but he is also
no alien to the goodness, truth and beauty of the realm of the
spirit. He lives by bread, but he also lives by verities of faith,
hope and love. Up to a point, he is governed by hunger and
pain, but he can and frequently does go beyond their limitations, defying them even to the death of the body because
his soul is at home in two worlds.

The pessimist likewise encounters an insurmountable wall
when he attempts to prove that life here is so miserable, so
cruel, so full of frustration, that life hereafter would not be
worth living even if it were possible. He is mute before the
affections of men which cry out against the severance of
death. Love, the most divine thing about man, flies in the
face of extinction and will not acknowledge defeat. Love is
supported by man's ethical sense, which refuses to admit
that the noblest lives are doomed to strive for lofty purposes
only to suffer mockery and frustration when they have but
begun to realize their aims. Love believes that those who

live up to their highest possibilities live for eternity. Love points out that justice is never fully satisfied in this life and that it is *right* to expect that our finite and temporal beginnings for good or ill shall find infinite and timeless fulfillment.

Finally, love holds that God is the God of the living, not of the dead. His gift of fellowship with men is the gift of life that can continue fellowship. He would not implant in his children a desire that is reasonable, moral and in harmony with the highest religious and social values, a desire that moves man to act in terms of his noblest ideals and worthiest aspirations, and then make the achievement of that desire impossible. No desire appears more universally among men than the desire for life after death.

God is known through the discovery of truth. The discovery of the whole truth concerning immortality will reveal to us, as does all other truth, that God is our Father. We need have no fear that if we knew all the truth concerning the life to come, that knowledge would cast the dark shadow of bottomless despair over our present life. Instead, we may go forward in confidence that "this slight momentary affliction is preparing for us an eternal weight of glory beyond all comparison" (II Cor. 4:15).

But our main dependence is not on rational defense of the hope of immortality. Even if such a defense were far more effectively made, it would still point only to a probability. And that is not enough. A generation which has known the tragedy of world wars and mass starvation and which now stands under the threat of wholesale extermination by atomic weapons needs something more. If it is to survive, it can do so only by standing in the living presence of him who is the resurrection and the life, who, being dead, yet speaks with the only kind of certainty that has any final meaning.

That certainty we find in the personal presence of the Lord Jesus Christ wherever it makes itself known, but supremely in the Eucharist. Today as in the upper room, Jesus sits at the head of the table speaking once more the familiar words. He is, as Brilioth says, "at every Eucharist the true celebrant," who is present "personally feeding his own with the sacred gifts, and imparting his own great gift, the forgiveness of sins and communion with God through him."* The testimony of Jesus Christ to life after death is conclusive, not in spite of the fact that it is received through faith, but because of it. Faith is an indispensable element in all intercourse between living persons. When we commune with Christ, we know as we could know in no other way that he lives—"knowing that he who raised the Lord Jesus will raise us also with Jesus and bring us with you into his presence" (II Cor. 4:13).

With this knowledge, we turn to the New Testament. There we are told that Jesus appeared first to Mary Magdalene, then to Simon Peter, then to the two disciples on the road to Emmaus, then to ten disciples. We are informed that a week later he was seen by all the disciples including Thomas, by seven on the Sea of Tiberias, by five hundred brethren at once, by James and by the apostles. Finally, he appeared to Saul of Tarsus. "It was not one person but many who saw him," said Paley, "not only separately but together, not by night only but by day, not at a distance but near, not once but several times; they not only saw him but touched him, ate with him, examined his person to satisfy their doubts." At the Lord's table, we see him today.

* Eucharistic Faith and Practice, p. 286.

There is another sense in which we encounter the living Christ at holy communion. He is in the elements themselves exactly in the way he was in them in the upper room. There he presided over the meal, giving his disciples bread and wine as symbols of his body and blood. At that time and place, as he sat in their midst, they had no difficulty in understanding his meaning. These elements were instruments of his self-communication. They were means by which the grace of his indwelling and living presence was conveyed to them. They were material vehicles through which spiritual truth was transmitted, and that truth was Christ himself. To the degree that they had faith to perceive him in the bread and wine, they became aware of life in themselves that was akin to the life that was in him.

It is just because of the simplicity and strength of this aspect of the Lord's Supper that it has suffered such distortion in history. The time was to come when a priesthood intent on consolidating its control over a superstitious people would use the words with which Christ conveyed this meaning to try to prove their own claim that they could convert bread and wine into the actual body and blood of Christ. When that happened, centuries later, the reality of the risen life for which the symbols stood had been forgotten. Then pride could cause a priest to say, as one is on record as saying: "We priests . . . occupy a position superior to that of the mother of God, who only once bare Christ, whereas we create and beget him every day. Yea, in a sense we stand above God, who must always and everywhere serve us and at the consecration must descend from heaven upon the mass."*

* As quoted by C. J. Cadoux, *Catholicism and Christianity* (London: George Allen & Unwin, Ltd., 1928), p. 404.

That no such idea was held at the end of the first Christian century is shown by the words of the Gospel of John—the very words which are most often lifted out of their context to support this view. The Gospel declares that Jesus said: " 'I am the bread of life. Your fathers ate the manna in the wilderness, and they died. This is the bread which comes down from heaven, that a man may eat of it and not die. I am the living bread which came down from heaven; if any one eats of this bread, he will live for ever; and the bread which I shall give for the life of the world is my flesh.'

"The Jews then disputed among themselves, saying, 'How can this man give us his flesh to eat?' So Jesus said to them, 'Truly, truly, I say to you, unless you eat the flesh of the Son of man and drink his blood, you have no life in you; he who eats my flesh and drinks my blood has eternal life, and I will raise him up at the last day. For my flesh is food indeed, and my blood is drink indeed. He who eats my flesh and drinks my blood abides in me, and I in him. As the living Father sent me, and I live because of the Father, so he who eats me will live because of me. This is the bread which came down from heaven, not such as the fathers ate and died; he who eats this bread will live forever.' This he said in the synagogue, as he taught at Capernaum" (John 6:48-60).

The book in which these words appear was the latest of the Gospels to be written. There is considerable doubt that they were spoken with reference to the Lord's Supper. The author of John's Gospel was influenced by Greek thought, which had strongly affected part of the church by the end of the second generation after Christ. But even though this strain of thought led eventually to the errors of transubstantiation, these words could have held no such connotation to the people of the generation in which they were written. Jesus was remembered to have been standing in the midst of the disciples when he made these statements. He was speaking in the present tense as well as of the future, and what he said must obviously be applicable to both. "I am the bread of life," said this living person as he stood before them, and no one took his words as an invitation to a cannibal feast. In exactly the same sense, he continues to be the bread of life today, and in no other.

There remains a third way in which the living Christ is present at the Lord's table. He is present in the fellowship of believers. The symbols represent not only his personal body but also his spiritual body, which is the church. Of that body all who accept him in faith as the Son of God are members. This conception predominates in the writings of Paul. "The cup of blessing which we bless, is it not a participation in the blood of Christ? The bread which we break, is it not a participation in the body of Christ? Because there is one loaf, we who are many are one body, for we all partake of the same loaf" (I Cor. 10:16-17).

The continuance of the fellowship of faith is itself a testimony to the continued life of Jesus Christ, the Head of the church. How otherwise can the trust of sixty generations be explained? Mankind is easily deceived, but it does not persist in a course of action for two thousand years without reason. In this instance, the reason is found in the corroborative evidence which is available to generation after generation that "you are the body of Christ and individually members of it." So the church unites in singing:

One Christ we feed upon, one living Christ,
 Who once was dead, but lives forever now;
One is the cup of blessing which we bless,
 True symbol of the blood which from the Cross did flow.

My life, my everlasting life art Thou,
 My health, my joy, my strength I owe to Thee;
Because Thou livest, I shall also live,
 And where Thou art in glory, there I too shall be.*

The truth is much greater than are the words with which we seek to express it. The truth about immortality is far more significant than any of the theories with which we attempt to convey our beliefs concerning the life that transcends death. So any formula of words must always be held in humility. We must realize that it stands under the judgment of a reality which far surpasses our capacity for expression. That reality is a living person. His name is Jesus Christ.

As we approach the Lord's table, we prepare ourselves for the encounter with Jesus through prayer in the best way we can. We cannot prepare ourselves at all, however, unless we do so in the faith which sees that it is Jesus Christ, our living Lord, whom we meet. Seeing him at the table, we receive the elements from his hands. We accept them as a means through which he chooses to communicate his grace. We commune with the fellowship of the faithful in the knowledge that Christ is the central figure, the power and the glory of the church. Thus, in knowing him whom to know is life eternal, we find in the Lord's Supper a monitor of immortality.

* Horatius Bonar.

Transubstantiation cannot be proved by Holy Writ. The body of Christ is given, taken and eaten in the Supper only after a heavenly and spiritual manner. And the means whereby the body of Christ is received and eaten in the Supper is faith. The Sacrament of the Lord's Supper was not by Christ's ordinance reserved, carried about, lifted up or worshipped.

28th Article of Religion of the Church of England

CHAPTER ELEVEN

Transubstantiation

IN THE preceding chapters we have discussed seven meanings of the Lord's Supper. This discussion was based on an assumption which was clearly stated : that the bread and wine of the communion have significance as physical symbols of spiritual reality. This assumption is immediately verifiable by the evidence of the senses aided by the normal processes of reason. It is sustained by the laws of nature. It is morally invigorating, intellectually satisfying, and spiritually fertile and rewarding. It is in harmony with what we know about the early Christian Church. It is consistent with all that the New Testament teaches about the life and purposes of Jesus Christ and the character of God our Father.

This discussion would not be complete, however, without an examination of the opposite point of view concerning the Lord's Supper. That is the position that the bread and wine of the Eucharist are not symbols, but at some point become the literal and actual body and blood of Jesus Christ. It is important for Christians who do not hold this view to understand how it came to be held by large sections of the church. Surely this can be done without impugning the good faith of those who, for reasons rooted in an imperfectly understood history, maintain a view which we believe to be demonstrably erroneous.

The literalist view of the eucharistic elements is called the doctrine of transubstantiation. It holds that priests of the Roman Catholic Church, by correct performance of the ritual of the mass, miraculously transmute the elements of the communion from bread and wine into the living flesh and blood of Jesus Christ, in which form they are received by the worshiper. The Roman Church formally defined this doctrine for the first time at the Fourth Lateran Council, which was convened by Pope Innocent III on November 11-30, 1215. The decree then issued stated: "There is one true universal church of the faithful, outside of which no one can be saved, in which Jesus Christ himself is the priest and sacrifice, whose body and blood are truly contained in the sacrament of the altar beneath the species of bread and wine, the bread being transubstantiated into the body and the wine into the blood by divine power, so that we receive for perfecting the mystery of unity from his very self that which he received from us. So no one can prepare this sacrament save the priest, who has been properly ordained according to the keys of the church which Jesus Christ himself gave to the apostles and their successors."

The position taken in 1215 was a contributing cause of the Protestant Reformation, which occurred three centuries later. The Reformation was followed by the Council of Trent, in which the hierarchy reaffirmed the Lateran decision on October 11, 1551, in the following words: "Through the consecration of bread and wine the conversion takes place of the whole substance of the bread into the substance of the body of Christ our Lord, and of the whole substance of the wine into the substance of his blood, which conversion is conveniently and properly called transubstantiation by the Holy Catholic Church."

How did it happen that this doctrine was not defined by a church council until the thirteenth century? What was the fate of the church scholars who had previously opposed this theory and maintained instead the position now held by most Protestant Christians? What forces contributed to the final victory of materialism in the Roman Church?

It is significant that the Lord's Supper did not become the subject of extensive debate in the church until the ninth century. The discussion arose then because a Benedictine monk named Paschasius Radbertus, in the first known book on the question, advocated the literal and materialistic view which had come to be held by some bishops and other church leaders. Writing in a spirit characteristic of those dark ages, Radbertus completed in 831 a volume, *Liber de Corpore et Sanguine Domini*, in which he identified the eucharistic body of Christ with his historical body. In the sanctification of the sacrament, he held, the bread and wine are changed by the Holy Spirit into the flesh and blood of Christ. This process he defined as the creation of "a new creature." His stark materialism shocked the conscience of many even in his own day, but it served what the bishops believed to be the interests of the church. In an age of general belief in miracles as a daily occurrence, it enabled the church to dominate people's minds by its monopoly on the wonder of all wonders, the creation at will of God himself.

Radbertus' book attracted little attention until 844, when he sent a revision of it to Charles II, Holy Roman emperor and king of France, otherwise known as Charles the Bald

(823-877). Charles was waging an often unsuccessful war against the feudal nobles, who were backed by the church. He may have seen in the Radbertian doctrine a further strengthening of the clergy and an encouragement to their encroachment on his dwindling authority. Whatever the explanation, he invited Ratramnus, a learned monk of the same abbey (Corbey on the Weser), to reply to Radbertus. Since the Corbey Benedictines were widely known in that day as expounders of Augustine, who held that the elements are symbols, Charles was not wholly disingenuous when he asked Ratramnus to answer two questions, which were really one: In the communion, are the body and blood of Christ received in a mystery which is perceived only by the eye of faith; or actually, so that the body and blood are seen by the bodily eye? Is the eucharistic body that which was born of Mary, suffered, died, was buried, rose again, ascended into heaven, and sits at the right hand of the Father?

Ratramnus wrote a book, *De Corpore et Sanguine Domini,* in which he refuted Radbertus by attacking his sources. Radbertus had built his case chiefly upon Ambrose (340-397), the bishop of Milan, who emphasized the idea of conversion of the elements. Ratramnus refuted Ambrose by quoting the latter's contemporary Augustine (354-430), who declared that "one thing is seen, another is understood," as a defense of the symbolic view. Augustine maintained that the bread and wine are the means of communicating the divine gift, but are always to be distinguished from the gift itself. "It is a miserable slavery of the soul to take signs for things and to be unable to raise the eye of the mind above the bodily creature to the eternal light," he said. In another passage he expresses this view with equal clarity: "Christ at the Last Supper instructed his apostles saying, 'Understand spiritually that which I have spoken; ye are not about to eat this body which ye see, nor are ye about to drink this blood which those men shall shed who will crucify me.'"

Ratramnus stated flatly that nothing is more absurd than to receive the bread as actual flesh and to say that the wine is actual blood. He gave a plain answer to Charles II by declaring that there is no identity between the eucharistic body and the historical body of Christ. He said that the substance which the bread and wine had before the consecration they possess after it, and emphasized Augustine's distinction between the sacrament and the thing of which it is the sacrament. The symbolism of the elements, however, is real, he said. Through it Christ imparts his grace and virtue.

What happened to Ratramnus? Nothing. Six centuries later, when the Reformation had taken up his ideas, his book was forbidden to Catholics and it remained on the *Index* until 1900. But during his lifetime he remained in the church. While his difference with Radbertus caused various church leaders to range themselves on one side or the other, the church tolerated both schools of thought, as it had done since the days of Ambrose and Augustine. Official policy, however, leaned to the side of the controversy which gave the clergy greater power. That was of course the materialist view, which handed them a monopoly on the supreme miracle and thus strengthened the immediate influence of the church.

This first eucharistic controversy simmered along for a couple of generations and then died away. By the time the second controversy broke out in the eleventh century, the hierarchy had become more sensible of the advantages of the materialist position. So when the great Berengar of Tours

(1000-88) espoused the doctrine of Augustine and Ratramnus, he was taken roundly to task and was tried repeatedly. Twice he was compelled to recant in Rome. But his chief biographer and commentator, A. J. Macdonald, maintains in his monumental *Berengar and the Reform of Sacramental Doctrine* that "he abjured the recantation of 1079 . . . There can be little doubt that the interpretation of the Eucharist which he had held for over forty years, for which he was condemned at fourteen synods and councils, and which he reaffirmed in his final polemical work after the Roman Council of 1079, was the faith in which he died."*

The reaction to Berengar's teachings revealed how far the trend within the church toward literalism had progressed in two centuries. Several facts account for this. The predominant one was the low level of culture. The people were grossly ignorant and the clergy were hardly less so. Both were ruled by those whose power was sustained by fashioning and exploiting popular superstitions. A second was the purging of the Benedictine order. In place of those who held to the stern intelligence of Augustine, leaders more amenable to the heads of the church were installed. A third was the way in which the bishops of the Roman Catholic Church fostered their growing authority by assiduous propagation of a eucharistic mythology based on the lowest form of materialistic literalism.

One of the stories which were widely circulated and gained general credence at this time concerned Pope Gregory the Great. When the pope gave a woman the host and said to her that this was the "body of our Lord Jesus Christ," she laughed because she saw only a small piece of bread. Gregory stopped the mass and exhorted her and the congregation. He and his

* London: Longmans, Green & Co., 1930; p. 221.

clergy then fell on their knees and prayed. When they rose all saw that the bread had become a piece of flesh.

Another story concerned a Jew, an unbeliever, who entered the church, saw blood in the chalice, saw that the host was flesh. When he told his wife, she was converted. Another Jew, a boy, went into a church with some other children and communed. His father heard about it and thrust his son into a furnace. The boy's mother got help and rescued him unharmed from the fire. The lad's explanation of his survival was that Mary, whom he said he had seen bear her little son into the church to be cut up for the sacrifice of the mass, had thrown her robe about him in the furnace. Frequently the linking of Jews with such stories provided the occasion for a pogrom in which whole colonies were dispossessed and slaughtered.

Berengar brought the wrath of the ecclesiastics down upon his head by denouncing this systematic exploitation of superstition. At least one of his books was destroyed on papal orders. His greatest book, however, *De Sacra Cœna,* survived, although in mutilated form. He was constantly under attack and replied with courage and insight to his detractors. His exposition was not without results, even though he did not receive credit for them. He compelled his opponents to relinquish the Radbertian doctrine that the body found in the communion was the historical body of Christ. He forced a repudiation of the crass statement of Humbert, his prosecutor before one of the councils, that the "true body and blood of Christ" were materially present in the Eucharist and that they were actually handled and broken by the priest and ground by the teeth of the faithful.

With relentless logic, Berengar linked the low estate of

religion in his time to the church's sanctification of error. In *De Sacra Cœna,* he described his day as one of apocalyptic depravity. "In the time in which it has pleased God that we should be born," he said, "we see the overthrow of religion, the sun turned into darkness, the moon into blood, when all confess that they know God, but deny him in their conduct, crying 'Lord! Lord!' but flying from his commands." He denounced the clergy as an ignorant mob.

Fortunately, Berengar had friends of high estate and low. The reigning pope once came to his rescue when he was harried by a prince, and he ended his days under the protection of former pupils. His cry for reform sought to bring the church back to Augustine and to a religious interpretation of the Scripture. He did not succeed in that. It would require the Reformation to bring a part of the church back to that position. In his own day, the chief results of his work were to reduce by a small degree the excesses of superstition and to raise questions which later generations were to answer.

One of the consequences of Berengar's resolute protest was a revival of interest in intellectual pursuits. Most of this was channeled into the direction of Scholasticism, which was just over the horizon, but not all of it. Bernard of Clairvaux, Abelard, and Anselm are among those whose writings reveal Berengar's influence. As usual, however, action produced reaction. This took forms which resulted in further externalization of religion. During the eleventh, twelfth, and thirteenth centuries, the elevation of the host in the mass was introduced, later to be signalized by the ringing of the bells; processions on Palm Sunday and on Corpus Christi day, which now began to be widely observed, were started; and kneeling in adoration of the host was decreed, although "kneeling with a view to adoration of the elements was unheard of in the primitive church," according to F. W. Conybeare. About 1100, communion in one kind was introduced. Up to that time laymen as well as priests received both elements. After the Council of Constance in 1415, in the Roman Catholic Church only the priest could commune in the New Testament sense.

During the twelfth century, Berengar's philosophical challenge brought about the invention and popularization of certain words which were to play their part in history. It was at this time that "transubstantiation" first came into use. It was probably invented by Hildebert of Tours in 1079, although E. C. Ratcliffe maintains that it was first used by Peter Daminni in 1072. Somebody began to apply the Aristotelian doctrine of substance and accidents to the elements of the Lord's Supper. The miracle of the mass, it was contended, changes the substance or inner universal quality of the bread and wine into the actual body and blood of Christ, while the accidents or sensible outer properties of the elements continue to be those of bread and wine. A little later the church agreed for the first time that there are seven sacraments, not five as Abelard held, or two, or ten. About the same time Peter Lombard taught that the sacraments "contain" grace and that they are "causes of grace" regardless of the faith or lack of faith of the recipient or the moral fitness or unfitness of the priest who administers them.

Thus a growing exteriorization led the church step by step away from its true function to witness to the gospel as it is in Jesus Christ and into the wastes of materialism, literalism and superstition.

This trend bore its decisive fruit at the Fourth Lateran

Council in 1215, which determined Catholic thinking and practice concerning the mass from that time until now. In addition to the doctrinal factors already mentioned, the political situation influenced the Lateran meeting. Pope Innocent III had started his Albigensian Crusade a few years before, and it was going badly. The Albigensians flourished, as they did especially in France, partly as a consequence of the decay of the spiritual life of the church, and particularly because they could no longer endure the oppression of a corrupt clergy. In their revolt against this corruption they outlawed the mass altogether.

At the time of the Fourth Lateran Council, it was still uncertain whether the Albigenses could be stamped out. The pope looked at the sad state of the Catholic faith and the threatened disintegration of the papal power and decided that more rigorous disciplines were called for. So he got the approval of the council for the confession of faith which is quoted on the third page of this chapter. It was no accident that in this confession the materialist conception of the mass was linked with the totalitarian idea of the church. Each required the other for support. At that moment in history, considerations of political and ecclesiastical power converged with a situation of spiritual demoralization which was the outcome of centuries of deepening ignorance, superstition and false doctrine to produce a result catastrophic for Christianity.

Following the Fourth Lateran Council, Scholasticism frittered away whatever chance may have remained for the Roman Catholic Church to recover its mission. Instead of attempting to recall the church to its pristine strength as a spiritual leaven in society, Thomas Aquinas and his successors exhausted their energies and abilities in ever more intricate refinements and elaborations of the arguments advanced by the literalists from the days of Cyprian and Ambrose onward. To provide a rationale for the new practice of communion in one kind, Aquinas taught that the whole Christ was present entirely in each species (element) of the communion and in every fragment of each species. Caught in the narrow limitations of legalism, he added nothing of importance to the thought of Christendom on the communion, but gathered up, systematized and rationalized the contributions of his pre-Lateran predecessors.

One of Aquinas' most difficult problems was how to explain the accidents. Why should the form and properties of bread and wine persist after they had become the actual body and blood of Christ? His answer, as found in the *Summa Theologicæ*, III, 75:5, is typical of the tendency of Scholasticism to depend on rhetoric instead of reason: "First, because it is not customary but horrible for men to eat the flesh of a man and to drink his blood, the flesh and blood of Christ are offered to us under the form of things which are more frequently used, namely, bread and wine. Secondly, lest this sacrament might be ridiculed by unbelievers if we ate the Lord in his own form. Thirdly, that while we receive the body and blood of our Lord, this may contribute to the merit of our faith." To set such rationalizing in its proper light, we have only to note how remote its terminology is from the accents and spirit of the upper room.

Once transubstantiation was officially adopted, it was only a step to the affirmation that the real presence of Christ is impossible without transubstantiation. Then the voices in the church which in each generation had insisted on the validity of the spiritual and symbolic view of the communion began to ring with new urgency. They gave abundant advance warning of the coming of the Reformation, but unfortunately there was nobody capable of hearing them.

Wyclif, for example, denied transubstantiation, exposed the inconsistencies and shallowness of the Scholastics, and attacked the abuses of church administration. He did not hesitate to charge with idolatry participants in the mass as now conceived. He flew in the face of church authority to insist that a sacrament celebrated by an unworthy priest was not valid. Elsewhere in Europe, John Hus spoke out against the innovation which denied the communion cup to the laity, and the Waldensians revolted against the church as it was and attempted to return to the simplicity of New Testament faith. The rulers of the church replied with increasing bitterness and ever more severe repressive measures, and before long were burning heretics at the stake.

The original purpose of the Lord's Supper was now largely lost beneath an accumulation of traditions which made the observance a sacrifice of appeasement of a God who was very different from the God and Father of Jesus Christ. Through this propitiatory sacrifice the church claimed to mediate salvation by means of an elaborate system of rewards and penalties. God had become a distant deity who had turned over to the church the administration of a system of sacrificial law. The church ruled the lives of the people through its priests. The practice of priestly imposition of penances, originating in Ireland, spread throughout the church. The growth of this order of rewards and penalties was gradual but certain. At its center was the mass.

God's wrath against mankind—so the theory ran—could be appeased only by the death of his Son. Since the mass was declared to be a repetition of Christ's sacrifice on Calvary, it followed that the multiplication of masses was the surest protection against the penalties of sin. The Roman Church taught—and teaches—that the accumulation of a treasury of masses furnished inexhaustible resources of "merit" for buying off God. The sale of indulgences in the open market was only the capsheaf of the corruption which, as a result of the perversion of the Lord's Supper, pervaded the entire system of religious belief and practice.

Seen against this background the Reformation was inevitable. Indeed it began on the inside, with repeated calls for the church to repent. The church met those appeals by attempts at repression, and when these failed (because the historical circumstances made extermination of dissenters impossible) it cast out those who might have been the instruments of its own reformation. Every Christian must regret this event, especially in the light of the divisions that resulted from it. But tragic as were the consequences, they were less tragic than would be the state of Christendom if the system which had taken the place of the religion of Jesus Christ had prevailed universally.

The Council of Trent, which convened a generation after the Reformation began, asserted "in defiance of history," as Harnack says, "that it has always been unanimously confessed by all the Fathers that the God-man is present 'truly, really, and substantially under the form of things sensible.'" It reaffirmed the Radbertian doctrine, as refined by the Scholastics, in the form devised by the Fourth Lateran Council and cited earlier in this chapter. It attempted to include Augustine in its fellowship by declaring that the Eucharist is a "symbol of a sacred thing and the visible form of invisible grace," but promptly negated this concession by saying that "other sacraments only have power to sanctify when someone uses them, while in the Eucharist, the sacrament is itself the author of sanctity previous to its use." In other words, the elements are not symbols, but are Christ himself.

Trent met the challenge of the reformers by anathemas. It anathematized anybody who does not see the whole Christ corporeally in the sacrament, anybody who denies that the whole Christ is present in every part of each element, anybody who rejects the worship of the host. "If anyone shall say that faith alone is sufficient preparation for taking the sacrament of the most holy Eucharist, let him be accursed," it declared, and condemned those who say that forgiveness of sins is the principal fruit of the Eucharist. It pronounced maledictions on those who demand the cup "as commanded by God" or question the right of the church to withhold the cup from the laity if it chooses to do so. Although there is no trace in Christian literature until the twelfth century of the claim that there are exactly seven sacraments, the council decreed that exactly seven sacraments were instituted by Jesus Christ.

When the Council of Trent finally adjourned after its third session in 1562-63, it left the Roman Catholic Church saddled with a complete system of religion based on a materialistic rite, the mass. "The changes imposed on the Christian religion by Catholicism," says Harnack, "are at no point so obvious and far-reaching as in that of sacrifice and especially in the solemn ordinance of the Lord's Supper. . . . In the whole history of religions there is probably no second example of such a transformation, extension, demoralization, and narrowing of a simple and sacred institution." It was his verdict that the mass had become "sacramental magic in its coarsest form."

Perhaps the best summary of the case against transubstantiation has been made by a member of the Society of Friends in Britain. In his excellent book, *Catholicism and Christianity*, Cecil John Cadoux declares that "the Roman idea of transubstantiation is simply not to be found in the earliest centuries" of the church. Catholic eucharistic doctrine does violence to the plain meaning of the Scriptures, he says; it presupposes and depends upon the highly questionable metaphysics of the Scholastics, which distinguishes between the "accidents" or perceptible qualities of a thing and its underlying "substance." Bread and wine become the "substance" of the actual body and blood of Christ, retaining meanwhile the "accidents" of their appearance as bread and wine. This is untenable. On the other hand, transubstantiation is not necessary to the use of the Eucharist as a means of grace.

Again, Cadoux remarks, the Catholic view opens wide the gate to all sorts of abuses, sins and errors. It requires that Jesus and his apostles shall be made priests in the same sense that the Catholic Church views the priesthood. "If, as Catholic theory demands, the passage [in I Cor. 11] limits to priests the right of administering the sacrament, it also limits the right of participation to the same class for the words, 'Take and eat,' were addressed to none but the apostles." The Roman catechism imports into the administration of the cup and places in Jesus' mouth words which are false and unscriptural when it requires the priest to say, "This is the cup of my blood, of the new *and eternal* testament, *the mystery of the faith,* which will be poured out on behalf of you and of many for the remission of sins."

Cadoux observes further that the Roman Catholic Church attempts to make the mass a true sacrifice of Christ himself, holding the rite to be not a dramatization but an actual extension and part of the sacrifice on Golgotha. Christ therefore becomes a perpetual victim and God an ogre who can be propitiated only by offerings forever renewed of living flesh and blood. Thus the priest is put in position to compel God to dance attendance on him, since God must always on command descend from heaven upon the mass. Finally, Cadoux declares, the church exceeds its rightful prerogatives when it withholds the cup from the laity, requires people to take the sacrament before other food, permits the reservation of the sacrament, and requires the saying of masses, in return for payment, on behalf of the dead in purgatory.*

The writer of these pages agrees with this appraisal, but would express his own view in words somewhat different from those of Cadoux. In his opinion, transubstantiation is impossible to reconcile with the evidence of the senses, which are given us by God to present their own testimony to our apprehension of the truth. It is contrary to the laws of nature, which is God's creation. It is intellectually stultifying, being an offense against sound reason through which we may know the will of God. It is morally debilitating, since it portrays God as acting in a way which would be regarded as reprehensible by any accepted ethical code, and therefore encourages actions on the part of his children which violate the moral law. It is spiritually deadening, because it erects an ecclesiastical and ideological barrier through which the love of God for his children and their love for him must pass. That love often passes this barrier cannot be denied, but that fact represents a tri-

* Catholicism and Christianity, (London: Allen & Unwin, Ltd., 1928) pp. 408 ff.

umph of the grace of God, occurring in spite of rather than because of transubstantiation.

With this in mind, we may yet agree with Cadoux's wise and temperate judgment: "The Catholic view of the Eucharist, though it commands our sympathy and deep respect in so far as it helps to bring home to people the nearness and graciousness of God through Christ, is yet associated with and in large part dependent upon a considerable number of clear historical errors, with which the equally sacramental and more authentic communion service of Protestants is happily unencumbered."

He who without faith approaches the Sacred Table, albeit he communicate in the sacrament, yet he perceives not the matter of the sacrament, whence is life and salvation.

HELVETIC CONFESSION, 1566, repre-
senting the view of John Calvin

CHAPTER XII

One Loaf—One Body

*Because there is one loaf, we who are many are
one body, for we all partake of the same loaf.*
                              —I Corinthians 10:17
*Now there are varieties of gifts, but the same
Spirit; and there are varieties of service, but the
same Lord; and there are varieties of working, but
it is the same God who inspires them all in every one.*
                              —I Corinthians 12:4-6

WORLD COMMUNION SUNDAY was inaugurated in
1940. Every year since it was first proposed by the Federal
Council of the Churches of Christ in America, churches
throughout the earth have observed communion together on
the first Sunday in October. The observance had only a brief
time to become established before World War II engulfed
mankind, but even during the war it was kept, at least to
some degree, on both sides of the battle lines. In Korea it
brought imprisonment and persecution to many Christians.
When it was discovered that they were praying in concert
with their brothers of the faith in other parts of the world,
the occupying authorities accused them of treasonable activity.
Now that the World Council of Churches may assume spon-

sorship of World Communion Sunday, it seems likely that
this observance will become an important addition to the
calendar of the Christian year.

It should be recognized as such. It offers to Christians of
all lands and of every variety of "gifts . . . service . . . working" an opportunity to proclaim the solidarity of the Church
of Christ. While the church's divisions are a fact which we
may never cease attempting to overcome, its unity is also a
fact which must be held in remembrance and continually
magnified. "We who are many are one body, for we all partake of the same loaf." That is as true today as when Paul
wrote it nineteen centuries ago. Those who are called to bear
witness to the truth may not neglect to give their testimony
concerning this often forgotten truth.

So far as the author of these pages is aware, the observance
of World Communion Sunday is the first and as yet the
only action in which a considerable share of the 137,000,000
Protestants on earth consciously and simultaneously affirm
their unity. They do so in thankful recognition that everywhere, as the earth turns on its axis to bring one land after
another to face the sun, Christians lift their eyes to the Son
of God in acknowledgment of a fellowship which includes all
who take the name of Christ. Because this universal observance
is nearest to the inclusive intention of our Lord, this should
be the most meaningful communion of the year. On this day
the walls of the upper room melt away and we all sit at table
with the Master.

World Communion Sunday takes a step in the direction
toward which every observance of the Lord's Supper points.
Its affirmation of Christian solidarity is certain to strengthen
in Protestants a sense of common life, of mutuality, of holy

fellowship in the Church of Christ. Its wide extension will be rich in the fruits of the Spirit.

Protestants should openly recognize that this action of ours is all that is required to unite Christendom in corporate worship before the throne of grace. The Roman Catholic and Orthodox churches already celebrate the Eucharist every day or at least every Sunday. When we agree on a universally accepted day, we complete the circle. This simultaneous achievement of Protestant unity and of global Christian action is an event of importance. Its significance is dimmed but not extinguished by the fact that unity of action does not connote full fellowship or cooperation so long as considerable sections of the Christian community are estranged from each other. Its importance chiefly lies in the acknowledgment each makes that Jesus Christ stands at the head of the table. We all confess that our only hope of partaking of eternal life rests in our Lord. In devotion to him and in commitment to his purposes, we take our places in his church. The day will come when we will recognize that in Christ is our unity as well as our freedom and our peace.

Bishop Brilioth, one of the modern scholars who have thrown most light on the Lord's Supper, never permits his readers to forget this fact. He says: "Our faith must be sufficient to be certain, as we can be certain, that this holy rite stood from the very beginning at the center of the stream of spiritual life which had its source in the Master himself and which is itself the chief witness to the power which was in him. And the place which the holy rite has held throughout all Christian history as the means to the communication of the Christ-life and of fellowship in Christ remains as a fact which no psychological subjectivism can explain away. Faith sees here the activity of the ascended Lord, continuing and confirming the work of his earthly ministry."*

Even more impressive are the words which appear in the message addressed to the churches of the world by the World Conference of Churches at the close of its meeting in Oxford in 1937. The solemn sense of impending global tragedy caused the conference to weigh its words to the churches with great care. "Despite our unfaithfulness," it said, "God has done great things through his church. One of the greatest is this, that notwithstanding the tragedy of our divisions and our inability in many important matters to speak with a united voice, there exists an actual world fellowship. Our unity in Christ is not a theme for aspiration; it is an experienced fact. We can speak of it with boldness because our conference is an illustration of it. We are drawn from many nations and from many different communions, from churches with centuries of history behind them and from the younger churches whose story covers but a few decades; but we are one in Christ. The unity of this fellowship is not built up from its constituent parts, like a federation of different states. It consists in the sovereignty and redeeming acts of its one Lord. The source of unity is not the movement of men's wills; it is Jesus Christ whose one life flows through the body and subdues the many wills to his."

These are great words. They should stir the postwar generation even more than they stirred that which stood under the shadow of World War II. The fact that the participants in the Oxford conference observed both the Orthodox and Anglican forms of the Eucharist, although they were prepared for communion in the same service, illustrates the difficulties

* *Eucharistic Faith and Practice*, p. 13.

which the life of Christ has in finding perfect expression through imperfect men. But it does not invalidate the truth that the Christian community is not divided at the source. We have only to follow our separate branches back to the trunk from which they draw their life to realize that He is the vine. We are all *branches*—a fact we too easily forget. Jesus Christ and he alone is the vine, the trunk, the living center of our unity.

"The source of unity," as Oxford said, "is Jesus Christ," not the Lord's Supper. Christian unity does not depend upon uniformity of administration of the Eucharist. The communion is a means—a principal means—which mediates to us the grace of the presence of Christ, but it is not the presence. That distinction must never be lost. We must hold it steadily before us if we are to understand the fact that the spirit of God continues to manifest itself through the Lord's Supper even in a divided church.

The World Conference of Christian Youth, which met in Amsterdam shortly before the outbreak of the Second World War, was not able to take communion in one body, but divided into four groups. Adherents of the Lutheran, Episcopalian, Orthodox and Reformed traditions each took the communion separately. That this should happen in a conference of young Christians, at least some of whom made strong efforts to prevent this appearance of disunity, is evidence of how difficult it is for men to overcome separatistic traditions. For if the young cannot find a way in which the Lord's Supper, one of whose meanings is the unity which is in Christ, may fulfill its purpose completely, there is little hope that their elders will do so.

Nevertheless, the Amsterdam conference powerfully felt

the unity which is in Christ, as the communion sermon of Robert Mackie indicates. "Jesus Christ," he said, "comes to our divided communions as Host. He takes our divided bread and blesses and breaks and gives. Whoever of us will be absent from any of these communion services, Jesus Christ will be there. They are not the services of the churches. It is His supper. Jesus Christ is always the Host. We love the communion services of our own churches, and none of us is quite at home elsewhere. But we can learn of Him from other services. . . . In this way we shall cease to have an idea of church unity made up of broken pieces which have lost their meaning. We shall be ready to work and to wait for the reunited church of our Lord Jesus Christ in all its fullness and splendor."

No concern of the Reformation has borne better fruit than its rediscovery of the meanings of the Lord's Supper to the disciples and the early church. In spite of lack of full agreement among Protestants themselves, the observance has once again become an expression of overflowing thanksgiving to God for the gift of his Son, a commemoration of Jesus Christ, whose living presence at his table is thus celebrated. Today the communion is an act of repeated renewal of the Christian's true covenant relationship with the Lord. It is a corporate acknowledgment of the church's fellowship with its living Head, a recognition of the source of spiritual nourishment and sustenance, a means of grace for the remission of sins and atonement with God, a fitting affirmation of life that continually widens its horizons to and beyond the grave.

An experience the author shared with a congregation of Chinese Christians in Nanking in 1940 remains in his memory as an illustration of the Lord's Supper as an expression of the unity and power of Christ. Perhaps four hundred people were assembled in the fire-scarred church. Two years before, their great city had fallen prey to an invading army, which had burned, looted and destroyed. They lived then under a pervasive and active tyranny. Not one person in the congregation was sure that on his way home from church that day he would not be killed or seized and tortured. Not one was secure in his property or could protect his family. All had had personal experience of the most flagrant injustice and all lived under conditions which would inspire terror in any people capable of terror.

But the atmosphere of this service was screne. The people sat there listening to the story of the upper room and to the deathless words of the communion service in their own language. They knew the presence of the living Christ even in tortured Nanking. In a city where salvation had a very present, individual and personal meaning, they lifted their voices in a hymn of thanksgiving for his saving grace. Then the elements were passed among them and they partook of them in a covenant never to forsake Him in whom they lived and through whom they were united with the ecumenical church. In the bread and wine their faith found sustaining strength from on high. And in that holy hour, these who lived in the valley of the shadow of death quietly reaffirmed the eternity of life with God.